Black
Pages 104 to 135
Here you will find minerals with a gray to black streak

Wh
Pag
Here
extre
that a ... the streak plate material

Magnetite

Ettringite

Galena

Rhodochrosite

Bournonite with siderite on quartz, from Neudorf in the Harz Mountains (Germany). The large crystal measures almost $2^1/2$ inches (6 cm) across.

Minerals

Rupert Hochleitner

**Identifying, learning about, and collecting
the most beautiful minerals and crystals**

500 color photos by the author and the staff of *Lapis*
300 drawings of crystals by the author
14 color drawings by Marlene Gemke

Contents

Crocoite crystals from Dundas (Tasmania). Size of crystals about ½ inch (1 cm).

◀ Cover photo: Rock crystal.
◀ Photo pages 2–3: Acicular kermesite crystals on
quartz, Braunsdorf near Freiberg (Saxony,
Germany); crystals up to 2½ inches (6 cm) long.

We humans have always been fascinated by minerals, crystals, and precious stones, and—as indicated by attendance figures for museums with mineralogical exhibits, mines that admit visitors, and mineral and gemstone shows—interest in these treasures from Earth's bowels continues to grow at a steady pace.

This Barron's guide is a new kind of book for identifying minerals, one that even beginners can use to make quick, sure identifications. Of the approximately 500 original photos presented here, about two thirds are new and have never before appeared in book form. The simple, easy-to-understand profiles are supplemented by sketches of crystals made by the author especially for this book and based on the most up-to-date crystallographic data. Barron's color key arranges the minerals according to the streak and the degree of hardness; identification thus becomes an easy matter, even for novices.

This new guide to minerals, however, is more than an aid to identification. The superb color photos, informative drawings, and descriptive profiles provide information about the appearance and properties of minerals and crystals, explain how they originated, and tell you where to find them.

In a section filled with practical advice, collectors of minerals are given various tips: Where to hunt for and find minerals, how minerals can be exchanged and bought, what field and home equipment a collector needs, and what criteria may be used in organizing a collection of minerals.

The author of this book and the editors of Barron's series of nature books hope you will enjoy your search for minerals and building a collection.

Tourmaline crystals from a pegmatite found at San Piero on the island of Elba (Italy). Crystals up to $1/2$ inch (1.5 cm) long. Such crystals, which are light-hued below (here, yellowish green) and tipped with black, are popularly known as Moor's-head tourmalines.

Learning About Minerals

On the following pages you will learn all about the properties of minerals—how they look; how hard they are; how to test the streak; how minerals are classified; how they originate; what is meant by tenacity; that form and habit are two entirely different things, although they are quite closely associated; and a great deal more.

What Are Minerals?

Minerals are naturally occurring chemical substances, uniform in terms of composition and, with one exception, of a solid consistency. The fact that they are naturally formed objects is quite important: Nothing made by man—from crystal glass to silicon crystal or artificial diamonds—is a mineral, even though it might otherwise fit the definition perfectly.

Crystals are solid chemical substances whose atoms are arranged in a uniform, regular pattern: They have a crystal lattice. As a rule, crystals are bounded by symmetrically arranged planar surfaces, the presence of which can be used to identify a crystal. Crystals may be of synthetic or of natural origin and those in the latter category are minerals as well. Crystal specimens that exhibit no smooth faces—either because faces were prevented from developing at all during the period of formation, or because they subsequently vanished as a result of weathering or some other mechanical or chemical stress—are called crystalline. Minerals whose atoms are not arranged regularly in the form of a crystal lattice are known as amorphous.

Quartz, for example, is crystalline and can form beautiful crystals, while opal, which is almost identical chemically, is amorphous. Crystals are automatically crystalline as well; crystalline minerals, on the other hand, do not necessarily form lovely, symmetrical crystals, and in that case the term massive is applied to them.

The Crystal-Chemical Classification of Minerals

Minerals are substances made up of one or more chemical elements. Experts assign them to groups on the basis of their chemical composition and structure.

This system of classification is used also by mineral collectors who want to arrange their collection systematically. Its advantage is that related minerals are placed near each other.

This grouping, however, is not suitable for use in a book on the identification of minerals, because crystal structure and chemical formula are not easily accessible diagnostic criteria for collectors.

Elements: Minerals that consist only of a single element are, for example, sulfur, graphite, diamond, and gold. This group also includes a number of quite rare, naturally occurring alloys.

Sulfides are compounds of sulfur with other elements (except oxygen), particularly metals—for example, pyrite (FeS_2), galena (PbS), and sphalerite (ZnS). This category also includes the corresponding compounds of elements with arsenic, antimony, bismuth, selenium, and tellurium—nickeline ($NiAs$), for example—and combined compounds—like arsenopyrite ($FeAsS$) or tetrahedrite ($Cu_3SbS_{3.25}$).

Halides are compounds of metals with the halogens fluorine, chlorine, bromine, and iodine—for example, fluorite (CaF_2) and halite, also known as rock salt ($NaCl$).

Oxides are compounds of elements with oxygen—for example, quartz (SiO_2), rutile (TiO_2), hematite (Fe_2O_3). Also in this category are the **hydroxides**, compounds of elements with the hydroxyl group OH^-—like goethite ($FeO(OH)$) and brucite ($Mg(OH)_2$).

**Topaz crystals from the ▶
Thomas Range in Utah, 10x**

Learning About Minerals

Sulfates are compounds of elements with the sulfate group $(SO_4)^{-2}$—for example, barite $(BaSO_4)$ and anhydrite $(CaSO_4)$. Also in this category are the **chromates**, such as wulfenite $(PbMoO_4)$, and the **wolframates** or **tungstates**, such as scheelite $(CaWO_4)$.

Carbonates are compounds of elements with the $(CO_3)^{-2}$ group, such as magnesite $(MgCO_3)$, siderite $(FeCO_3)$, and calcite $(CaCO_3)$. This category also includes the extremely rare **nitrates**, compounds of elements with the NO_3^- group.

Phosphates are compounds of elements with the $(PO_4)^{-3}$ group, such as triphyline $(LiFePO_4)$, monazite $(CePO_4)$, and xenotime (YPO_4). Also in this category are the corresponding compounds with arsenic, the **arsenates**, and with vanadium, the **vanadates**.

Silicates are compounds of elements with silicon and oxygen—for example, olivine $((Fe,Mg_2)[SiO_4])$ and kyanite $(Al_2[SiO_5])$.

The *rare organic compounds* comprise the final group—for example, whewellite $(Ca[C_2O_4] \cdot H_2O)$.

Mixed Crystals (Solid Solutions)

The structure of a type of crystal does not always adhere to an unvarying chemical formula. In siderite, for example, some portion of the iron atoms may be replaced by magnesium atoms. The guest component (magnesium) is distributed statistically or regularly within the crystal lattice of siderite. Crystals of this kind are called mixed crystals (solid solutions). They can form only if the components that substitute for each other are identical or similar in size. Thus, olivine is a mixed crystal made up of the magnesium silicate forsterite $(Mg_2[SiO_4])$ and the iron silicate fayalite $(Fe_2[SiO_4])$. Both these mineral species crystallize orthorhombically with the same type of lattice, and the magnesium and iron ions are

Photos: The phosphate apatite and the tungstate scheelite belong to different groups of the crystal chemical classification system for minerals.

Apatite, Fichtelgebirge (Germany), 2x

Scheelite, Tae-Wha (Korea), 1x

The Crystal Chemical Classification

Siderite, Brüderbund Mine, near Eiserfeld (Siegerland, Germany), 3x

almost identical in size. They form an unbroken solid solution series extending from one end member, forsterite, through all possible intermediate members to fayalite at the other end.

When certain compounds are able to blend completely, the dividing line usually is drawn at the 50 percent composition. If the composition of a mixed crystal hovers around this limit, only precise chemical analysis can tell you to which species of mineral the sample belongs.

Mixed crystals are quite common, because the molten mass or solution from which the crystals form contains a variety of substances that the growing crystal can use to construct its lattice.

Photo: Siderite, an iron carbonate, can also contain magnesium and manganese as mixed crystal components. The crystals shown here are associated with quartz and chalcopyrite.

The Properties of Minerals

If you are interested in identifying minerals, you need to have some knowledge of their properties. In the following pages, therefore, the most important properties are discussed. They also are listed in the individual profiles contained in the identification section of this book.

Hardness

Everyone is aware that crystals can be quite hard. Diamonds, for example, are used for cutting glass because of their considerable hardness. There are also very soft minerals, however, like talc, which can be easily scratched with your fingernail.

Talc and diamond are at opposite ends of the Mohs scale of hardness, according to which all minerals—with the exception of mercury, which is liquid—can be classified. Because the hardness is characteristic of a mineral species and is relatively easy to determine, it serves, along with the color of the streak, as a major diagnostic attribute. For this reason the minerals in this book are arranged, within each streak category, in order of increasing hardness.

By referring to the Mohs scale, collectors can determine the hardness of a mineral with sufficient accuracy for identification.

Mohs Scale of Hardness

The Mohs scale of hardness consists of a sequence of ten minerals, each of which will scratch the one that precedes it. To identify a specimen, take a mineral of intermediate hardness from the reference scale and test to see whether the unknown mineral can be scratched by it, or whether the reverse is true.

Depending on the result of this test,

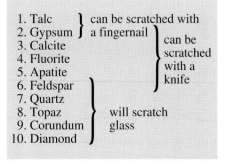

1. Talc } can be scratched with
2. Gypsum } a fingernail
3. Calcite
4. Fluorite } can be scratched with a knife
5. Apatite
6. Feldspar
7. Quartz
8. Topaz } will scratch glass
9. Corundum
10. Diamond

proceed with your efforts, using the next-harder or next-softer mineral and thus gradually defining the hardness of the unknown mineral. For approximate identification, especially in the field, you can rely on your fingernails (about hardness 2 on the Mohs scale), a pocket knife (hardness 5–6), and a piece of window glass (hardness 6–7).

Because the hardness of minerals is directional, or anisotropic, different values are obtained, depending on the direction in which the scratch is made. Generally, however, these differences are slight so the direction of the scratch is unimportant. But there are exceptions: The best-known example is kyanite, for which anisotropic hardness is so typical that it ranks as a diagnostic feature. Its bladed crystals yield a hardness of 4 to $4\frac{1}{2}$ on the Mohs scale if scratched lengthwise, or 6 to 7 if scratched crosswise.

Measuring the hardness of very small mineral specimens, the so-called

Photo: Native gold often forms very beautiful bizarre shapes. The specimen shown here comes from the Eagle's Nest Mine in California, and its actual size is about 2 inches (5 cm) in height. ▶

micromounts, is far more difficult. Because of their diminutive size, hardness cannot be judged by using minerals for comparison. Hardness can be at least estimated on the basis of the resistance that a mineral offers to a sharp-pointed steel needle, but this procedure requires the experience acquired only through numerous attempts.

For collectors, it generally is enough to determine a mineral's hardness according to the Mohs scale, as outlined before. If you want to obtain scientifically exact values, you will have to resort to more sophisticated methods.

The instrument most often used to determine absolute values is the sclerometer. In this method of measurement, the specimen is slid under a weighted steel or diamond pin. The pressure necessary to just barely scratch the mineral corresponds to the hardness of the mineral. The harder the mineral is, the greater the pressure that has to be applied to create a furrow.

How to Test the Hardness

- In a shop that sells mineral specimens, buy the minerals listed on the hardness scale. They are available for about $30, if you don't buy the diamond. However, because everything not scratched by corundum (hardness 9) can be scratched only by the diamond, you can get by with only nine minerals.
- It is best to begin by scratching the unknown material with fluorite. If that works, continue the test, using minerals of lesser hardness, until the unknown mineral no longer can be scratched. Then your specimen is somewhat harder than the last-used mineral from the Mohs scale. If it cannot be scratched with fluorite, take the next-harder mineral from the scale, until you find a mineral with which the unknown specimen can be scratched. The sample is then softer than the last-used mineral from the hardness scale.

Example: The unknown mineral is not scratched by feldspar (hardness 6); rather, it scratches the feldspar. Quartz (hardness 7), however, does leave a furrow. The hardness of the unknown mineral, therefore, is $6\frac{1}{2}$.

- Always test the hardness with sharp edges and in fresh places.
- Make sure that the mineral really has been scratched and that the mark resembling a scratch is not just powder from the test mineral. When the powder left by scratching is wiped away, a furrow has to be visible.
- With fine-grained mineral aggregates, the knocking out of individual little grains can simulate a lower hardness value. You need to pay even closer attention here.

Tenacity

As we have just learned, hardness is measured in terms of whether a mineral is scratched or not. The tenacity, or toughness, of a mineral, however, tells us something about the way it behaves when it is scratched and bent. As in the hardness test, the mineral is scratched, but this time with a steel needle. If the scratch dust drops away, the mineral is brittle. This is the case with the majority of minerals. Of particular importance in making identifications, therefore, are the properties that are less common:

Nonbrittle: A mineral is not brittle if the powder does not drop away when the scratch is made, but stays right next to the furrow. This is the case with galena and stibnite, for example.

Sectile: A mineral is sectile, or capable of being cut, if the needle penetrates and leaves behind a furrow without creating any dust. Examples are native bismuth, argentite, and native gold. Argentite and native gold can, in addition, be hammered out thin; they are **malleable** (ductile).

Flexible and elastic minerals, after being bent, return to their original shape. In this category are, for example, mica,

Hardness, Tenacity, and Density

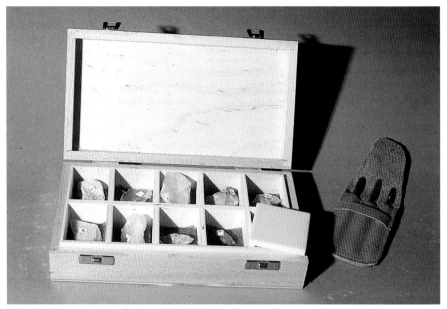

Scale of hardness, steel points for determining hardness, and streak plate

muscovite, and biotite.

Flexible but inelastic minerals, on the other hand, retain the new shape after they have been bent. Examples are gypsum and stibnite.

How to Test the Tenacity
- Using a sharply pointed steel needle, scratch the mineral you are trying to identify.
- Do not remove the scratch dust.
- Examine the furrow with a magnifying glass or a stereomicroscope.
- Test to determine whether the mineral is flexible.

Density (Specific Gravity)
Minerals can be heavy or light. Naturally you can tell the difference only with pieces of approximately the same size. A piece of gypsum as big as a hand, for example, is considerably lighter than a piece of pyrite the same size.

Although density and specific gravity

Photo: Determining hardness with the hardness scale or with steel points (only for hard minerals) and determining the streak with the streak plate are the basis of every mineral identification.

are different concepts, they will be treated as virtual synonyms in this book. Density (g/cm^3) is the term used to express the weight of a substance in proportion to its own volume. With the same mineral the density remains constant within narrow limits, no matter what the size of the specimen. If, for example, the density of a mineral is given as 13 in the descriptive profiles in this book, this means that one cubic centimeter of this mineral weighs 13 grams.

The density of almost all minerals is greater than 1, which means that they are heavier than water (at 39.2°F [4°C] water has a density of 1). The density of most minerals is between 2 and 3. Scheelite,

Learning About Minerals

barite, ore minerals, and native metals are substantially heavier.

In most cases, density ranges are reported in the profiles (for example, gypsum, 2.3–2.4; pyrite, 5.0–5.2), because the density of the individual aggregate forms varies. Usually the monocrystal (single crystal) has the highest density, while other aggregate forms yield lower values.

Collectors can determine density by lifting the unknown mineral in one hand and another mineral of known density and equal size in the other hand, then comparing the heft of the two minerals. In most cases that will be sufficient, although only approximate data are obtained with this method. The density of all ore minerals is a distinctive feature; they always feel heavy. The same is true of the minerals barite and scheelite, which will strike you as particularly heavy even when you merely try their weight in your hand. The low density of native sulfur, for example, is equally striking. Very small pieces, however, cannot be identified in this way. Experts, who are dependent upon accurate measurements of density, employ a hydrostatic balance, as well as other devices, when working with relatively large pieces. This balance is in universal use for determination of density. All the other methods are even more complicated and expensive, hence they normally are not applicable for collectors.

How to Test the Density
- Take the sample in one hand and determine whether it seems especially light or especially heavy to you.
- In your other hand, take a mineral of approximately equal size, whose density you know, and compare them.
- First, practice with pieces of known density.

Here are some density values for well-known minerals:

Sulfur	1.96
Quartz	2.65
Diamond	3.52
Hematite	5.30
Scheelite	6.10
Cassiterite	7.10
Uraninite	10.60

Photo: Silver-gray galena crystals along with some siderite, from Neudorf in the Harz Mountains (Germany). The largest crystal measures about ¹/₂ inch (1 cm). Ore minerals that contain an abundance of metal also have a high density, as you can tell just by holding them in your hand.

Characteristic: the Streak

Azurite, Schönbrunn (Vogtland, Germany), 5x

Amethyst, Mexico, 3x

Native gold	19.28
Native platinum	20.50

Streak

The streak of a mineral is the color of the trace left by the mineral when you rub it across an unglazed porcelain plate, the so-called streak plate.

The streak of a mineral is characteristic and hence is highly useful in identification. With monochromatic minerals (see Color, page 20), the color of the streak is the same as the body color of the mineral. Multicolored minerals, however, often have a streak whose color differs from the body color of the mineral.

Fluorite, for example, can occur in many colors, but its streak is invariably white. Minerals that are outwardly similar,

Photos: Multicolored minerals (like amethyst) have a white streak, while monochromatic minerals (like azurite) have a colored streak.

such as magnetite and chromite, can be differentiated with certainty by means of their streaks—black for magnetite, brown to yellowish brown for chromite.

Because the streak is one of the most important and most easily tested external features for identifying minerals, the identification section of this book groups minerals according to their streak.

Minerals that are harder than the material of the streak plate—that is, harder than 6—do not produce a true streak. They just scratch the streak plate

Learning About Minerals

Rhodochrosite crystals from the Wolf Mine (Siegerland, Germany), 6x

and leave behind a white trace of the streak plate material. In this book you will find all these minerals also included in the group of minerals with a white streak (arranged in order of increasing hardness).

How to Test the Streak
- In a store that sells mineral specimens, buy a streak plate; it will cost about $1.25. If need be, an unglazed porcelain fragment or a porcelain electrical fuse can also be used for this purpose.
- Rub the mineral against the plate. Compare the streak it leaves with the streaks of minerals in your collection that already have been identified.

Color
Identifying a mineral on the basis of its color seems quite simple at first glance. You don't need any complicated devices for this purpose; good light is enough. This applies, however, only to the so-

Photo: The beautiful red color and the interesting crystal form place the Wolf Mine rhodochrosites among the most unique in Europe.

called monochromatic minerals. An azurite from Tsumeb in Namibia is just as blue as the same mineral from Bisbee in the United States or from Neubulach in Germany's Black Forest. In these cases the color is characteristic of the mineral and thus is an important identifying attribute.

Multicolored minerals, however, cannot be identified by their color. In these cases the color is not characteristic of the mineral species, but is determined by minute amounts of foreign elements or by defects in the crystal structure. Depending on the locality, a multicolored mineral has various colors, sometimes even in the same specimen. Fluorite, for example, can occur in shades ranging

Monochromatic and Multicolored Minerals

from colorless through white, pink, yellow, brown, green, and blue to blackish violet.

In the profiles, terms from our everyday vocabulary were used for the color nuances. Here you have to allow for the fact that color impressions vary from one person to another. One observer, for example, may feel that something is green, while someone else would call it blue-green. Here too, however, collectors will quickly gain experience by making comparisons with minerals that already have been identified.

When determining a color, remember that some minerals—bornite, for example —may be covered with an oxidation coat of a color markedly different from that of the mineral. For this reason, it is essential to test the color at a fresh point of fracture.

How to Determine the Color
- Observe the mineral in strong light, ideally in daylight.

- Make sure you are really looking at the color of the mineral, not the color of an oxidation layer. If in doubt, test the color at a fresh point of fracture.

Luster
From time immemorial, gems have fascinated people because of their radiant luster. It is not only cut and polished precious stones, however, that are capable of reflecting light: Every rough mineral also has its own distinctive luster, as shown, for example, by the tiny flakes of mica in river sand. Luster is not measurable; it is described by comparisons with familiar things. This is, of course, a drawback, because it means that the diversity of the

Photos: Fluorite can occur in an enormous range of colors. It is not unusual even to find several colors in one specimen. The streak, however, is invariably white.

Fluorite, violet, Fichtelgebirge (Germany), 2x

Fluorite, rose-pink, New Mexico, 2x

Learning About Minerals

luster of minerals can never be described fully. You can compensate for this disadvantage, however, through experience, constant practice, and comparisons with already-identified minerals.

Experienced collectors will be able to state that the specimen in front of them cannot possibly be a certain mineral "because the luster isn't right," without being able to tell exactly why, however.

In this book the following types of luster are differentiated:

Vitreous luster corresponds to the luster of simple window glass.

Pitchy luster is seen, for example, in the freshly broken lumps of tar visible where road construction work is underway.

Minerals with a **silky luster** display a rippling gleam like that seen in raw silk.

Pearly luster reminds us of the inner layer of many shells (mother-of-pearl, or nacre) that has a whitish shimmer with a colored gleam.

Adamantine luster is the radiant luster that we know from cut diamonds and lead crystal glass. When minerals of this brilliance are colored yellow or brown, they produce a **resinous luster**.

Greasy luster reminds us of shimmering spots of grease on waxed paper.

Metallic luster corresponds to the luster of polished metal (as in car bumpers, jewelry, aluminum foil, etc.).

How to Determine the Luster

- Observe the mineral in strong light, if possible in bright daylight. Avoid yellow light, which can be deceptive.
- Turn the mineral back and forth; the characteristic luster often is visible only in a certain position relative to the light.
- Test the luster only on fresh specimens with a flawless exterior; do not use pieces that are oxidized or dirty.
- Compare the luster with that of minerals that already have been identified.

Cleavage and Fracture

Cleavage and fracture are two properties that can be tested simultaneously.

Cleavage describes the form of the fragments obtained by breaking the mineral with a hammer. The mineral may display smooth, flat cleavage planes or fall apart into regular, geometric bodies. Galena, for example, breaks into small cubes, calcite into little rhombohedrons. In the profile of the former mineral, under the heading Cleavage appears "highly perfect cubic"; for the latter mineral, it reads "along basic rhombohedral planes." The cleavage may exhibit various degrees ranging from "highly perfect" to "not discernible." Some minerals have no cleavage at all. In some cases the so-called cleavage angle, the angle at which the cleavage planes intersect, is also important for the purpose of identification. Pyroxenes, for example, have a cleavage angle of about 90°, which distinguishes them from the often very similar amphiboles, which have a cleavage angle of 120°.

Fracture, on the other hand, refers to all the surfaces of separation that are not cleavage planes. The fracture planes may be of various types, including conchoidal, or shell-like (quartz and obsidian), uneven (feldspar), and hackly, or jagged (gold).

These descriptive terms all are drawn from everyday language and thus need no further explanation. In the profiles, the form of the fracture planes is described after the cleavage.

In minerals with especially good cleavage, fracture is often difficult to detect.

How to Test Cleavage and Fracture

- Carefully break a sample of the mineral under investigation.
- Look at the resulting fragments, if necessary with a magnifying glass.
- Look for regular cleavage planes.
- If cleavage planes are present,

Cleavage and Fracture

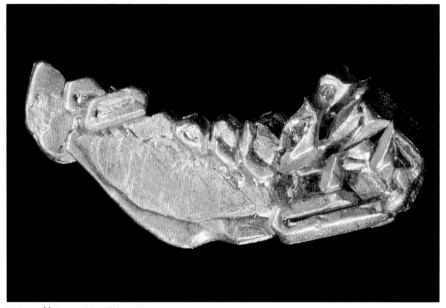

Native gold, Papua, New Guinea, 5x

determine their quality and possibly the angle at which they intersect (use a goniometer).

• If cleavage products have been created, determine their form. Look at the nature and form of the fracture planes and compare them with those of minerals that already have been identified.

Optical Properties

The behavior of light as it travels through a crystal is often used in mineralogy in the identification of minerals. However, this almost always requires equipment that collectors normally do not possess. For this reason, optical methods are extremely limited in their applicability for collectors, because the effects often are minimal at best and therefore not perceptible without instruments. Nevertheless, the most important concepts, with which even collectors need some familiarity, are explained as follows:

Photo: Native gold is the outstanding example of metallic luster.

Refraction of light: The rays of light are "bent" when they pass from one medium (air, for example) into another (a crystal, for example). The greater the difference between the two media, the more intense is the refraction. One measurement for the intensity of the refraction of light is the refractive index, which is abbreviated as n.

Birefringence or double refraction: A light ray that travels through a crystal of calcite is broken up into two rays, which travel in planes that are perpendicular to one another. The so-called ordinary ray travels in a straight line through the crystal, while the other ray, known as the secondary ray, is bent. If the incidence is oblique, both rays are deflected with varying intensity; that is,

23

the refractive indices for the two rays are different. This phenomenon is called birefringence or double refraction. It is most clearly seen in the case of calcite, but under a microscope it can also be detected in all other minerals, with the exception of those that are isometric (cubic) and amorphous.

Pleochroism: With anisotropic minerals—that is, all minerals except those that are isometric and amorphous —the absorption of the incident light in the different directions is also different. We see different colors, depending on the side from which we view the crystal. This phenomenon, termed pleochroism, sometimes can be seen with the naked eye in cordierite and some chlorites. In other minerals it is discernible only on a slide under a microscope.

Radioactivity

Elements that are not stable, but change into another element when alpha, beta, or gamma rays are emitted, are known as radioactive.

Alpha rays are helium atoms with a double positive charge (He^{2+}).

Gamma rays are electromagnetic waves characterized by a very short wave; they penetrate matter best, while alpha rays are quickest to be weakened and absorbed.

Beta rays are electron rays.

The radioactivity of a mineral specimen can be determined with a Geiger counter, a device for measuring radioactive radiation.

The most common radioactive elements found in nature are uranium and thorium. They are components of some minerals —for example, uraninite, torbernite, and autunite (uranium); and thorite, thorianite, and brannerite (thorium).

The radioactive elements of a mineral can, by means of their radiation, more or less destroy the crystal lattice. The mineral in question becomes amorphous and glasslike—metamict, as experts say.

The external crystal form remains intact, but the minerals become opaquely black-ish, the cleavage decreases, a greasy, pitchy luster appears, and the fracture becomes conchoidal. This is the case with samarskite, euxenite, gadolinite, and zircon, for example.

Pointers on Dealing with Radioactive Material

- Never store radioactive minerals in rooms that are inhabited.
- Collect only small specimens; larger pieces have to be shielded with lead.
- If you have touched radioactive substances, wash your hands carefully without delay.
- Don't eat and smoke while you are handling a radioactive substance.
- Store radioactive minerals out of the reach of children.

Fluorescence

If you irradiate minerals with ultraviolet (UV) light, you will see that a few mineral specimens glow more or less brightly in a great variety of colors. This phenomenon is known as fluorescence. Depending on the wavelength (we distinguish between long-wave and short-wave ultraviolet radiation), different colors may appear on the same specimen. Some minerals become luminescent only in long-wave, others only in short-wave UV light.

As a rule, fluorescence is not an original property of a certain mineral; rather, it is contingent upon the incorporation of certain elements into the crystal lattice—elements that do not inherently belong to the mineral. It may be that specimens of a mineral from some localities do not fluoresce at all, while specimens from other localities are intensely luminescent. Depending on the locality, a mineral can also fluoresce in a variety of colors.

If you turn off the source of UV light, in some minerals you can observe still another special property: After the light

Radioactivity and Fluorescence

Torbernite, Bergen (Vogtland, Germany), 6x

has been switched off, they continue to be luminescent for several seconds, usually in a color other than the fluorescent color. This property is called phosphorescence.

Collecting UV minerals is a popular hobby, but it is one that demands a certain amount of equipment and financial resources (building a special glass display case for UV minerals and buying a UV lamp—the lamps start at about $125). Then, however, there is no need to hunt for especially attractive and well-crystallized minerals, because in this case the fluorescent color and the size of the luminescent area are what matters.

How to Use UV Light
• Never look into the light source;

Photo: Danger! Uranium minerals are radioactive; despite their beauty, it is best not to collect them.

short-wave UV radiation in particular will damage your eyes irreparably in a very short time.
• Always wear protective goggles (available for only a few dollars).

The External Appearance of Minerals

When you look at crystals, fluorite or quartz, for example, you are struck by their completely smooth, flat contact surfaces. By comparing several crystals of a single mineral species, you can recognize that regardless of the size of the crystals, the angles between two like faces (measured perpendicular to the edge) are always the same. With crystals of different mineral species, however, that need not be the case.

Crystal Classes

All crystals, furthermore, are more or less symmetrical. A body is described as symmetrical if, by turning it or mirroring it (by symmetry operations, as experts say), we can bring it into a position that is indistinguishable from the previous one. The simplest symmetry operation is rotation of the crystal by 360°; if you yourself make a 360° turn—that is, turn completely around—you will again be in the position from which you started.

If you rotate a match box without a label, you will see that after a rotation of only 180° (semicircle) the box reaches a position that looks exactly like the initial one. To get the box back into the starting position, you have to turn it another 180°. This kind of symmetry operation is called twofold rotation.

Accordingly, the rotation angle for threefold rotations is 120°; for fourfold, 90°, and for sixfold, 60°. The axis around which the object is turned is called the rotation axis, or axis of symmetry.

In addition to these rotation axes, there is another symmetry element: The plane of symmetry, or mirror plane, which divides a crystal into two halves, each the mirror image of the other. At the center of a crystal lies the center of symmetry. It is responsible for the fact that for every face of the crystal there exists an opposite face at an equal distance from, but on the other side of, the center of symmetry. All these symmetry elements may appear in crystals singly or jointly. Overall, precisely 32 combinations of symmetry elements are possible. They correspond to the 32 crystal classes into which all crystals can be arranged. The minerals are not evenly distributed among these 32 classes; some classes contain many representatives of the mineral kingdom, while others include virtually none at all.

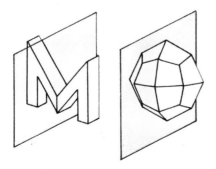

The plane of symmetry is a plane that divides an object into two halves, each a mirror image of the other.

Photo: Many minerals display forms ▶ that are immediately recognizable. Here, apatite's hexagonal prism with base (Pakistan), 2x.

Learning About Minerals

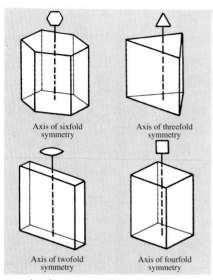

Axis of sixfold symmetry

Axis of threefold symmetry

Axis of twofold symmetry

Axis of fourfold symmetry

Examples of various axes of symmetry

Crystal Systems

The crystal classes are organized according to seven groups, the seven crystal systems (see also back foldout). The crystals in each system always have the same system of coordinate axes. For collectors only the seven crystal systems are important; the 32 crystal classes are best reserved for experts.

Isometric or cubic crystal system: System of axes with three axes of equal length and at right angles to each other.

In this system there are at most three axes of fourfold symmetry, four axes of threefold symmetry, six axes of twofold symmetry, nine planes of symmetry, and one center of symmetry.

A crystal belongs to the isometric system if at least two axes of threefold symmetry are present. This system is the most highly symmetrical.

Tetragonal crystal system: System of axes with two axes of equal length and one that is longer or shorter than the other two (the so-called c axis).

In this system there are at most one axis of fourfold symmetry, four axes of twofold symmetry, five planes of symmetry, and one center of symmetry.

A crystal is assigned to the tetragonal system if a single axis of fourfold symmetry is present. There must be no axis of threefold symmetry.

Hexagonal crystal system: System of axes with three axes of equal length, all on one plane and intersecting at an angle of 120°. These three axes are also intersected at right angles by a fourth axis (c axis) that is longer or shorter. This c axis is an axis of sixfold symmetry. In addition, there are six axes of twofold symmetry, seven planes of symmetry, and one center of symmetry.

A crystal is part of the hexagonal system if it has either one axis of sixfold symmetry or one axis of threefold symmetry with a plane of symmetry at a right angle to it.

Trigonal crystal system: System of axes as in the hexagonal system, except that the c axis now is an axis of threefold symmetry. In addition, there are three axes of twofold symmetry, three planes of symmetry, and one center of symmetry.

A crystal is included in the trigonal system if one and only one axis of threefold symmetry is present.

Orthorhombic crystal system: System of axes with three axes of unequal length, all at right angles to each other. In this system there are at most three axes of twofold symmetry, three planes of symmetry, and one center of symmetry. A crystal belongs to this system if at least two axes of twofold symmetry or at least two planes of symmetry are present. There must be no other axes of symmetry.

Monoclinic crystal system: System of axes with three axes of unequal length,

Crystal Systems

Japanese-law-twin, Val d'Aosta (Italy), 4x

two of which intersect at an acute angle, while the third is at a right angle to them. In this system there are at most one axis of twofold symmetry, one plane of symmetry, and one center of symmetry. A crystal belongs to the monoclinic system if it has only one axis of twofold symmetry and/or one plane of symmetry.

Triclinic crystal system: System of axes with three axes of unequal length, all of which are inclined at some angle other than 90°. In this system there is at most one center of symmetry. A crystal belongs to the triclinic system if neither axes of symmetry nor planes of symmetry are present. This system has the least degree of symmetry.

Photo: Because this particular twinned form of quartz was first discovered in Japan, these twins are known as Japanese-law-twins.

To describe the crystal faces precisely, experts use groups of three numerals called Miller indices. These three numerals, always enclosed in parentheses, give the inclination and the position of the face in question relative to the system of axes. To determine the Miller indices of a crystal face, you need exact goniometric measurements, which collectors normally cannot perform. For this reason, no detailed explanation of the indices is given here. The indices also

Learning About Minerals

are omitted from the identification section.

Characteristics of Crystals

Collectors need to be able to recognize the following characteristics of crystals; they are important diagnostic properties.

- **Form** is the term used for the set of all the faces present in a crystal, independent of their development and size.
- **Habit**, on the other hand, refers to the proportions of the individual faces of a crystal in relation to each other. Crystals with the same form (for example, a tetragonal prism with a base) may, depending on their growth habit, be tabular, isometric, prismatic, acicular (needlelike), or capillary (filiform or hairlike).
- **Twins** are two[*] individual crystals of the same crystal type that have intergrown in a regular association. Twins are often marked by the presence of reentrant angles, which cannot appear in individual crystals—although they are not necessarily present in twins. The Japanese-law-twin of quartz, for example, has reentrant angles, but they do not appear in the other twins of this mineral.
- Corresponding to the phenomenon of twinning, there also exist **trillings** (intergrowths of three individuals), **fourlings**, and, in general, **multiple twins**.
- With **polysynthetic twins**, twinning occurs repeatedly, creating fine twin lamellae that produce a striation on crystal faces.
- If crystals grow "floating," so to speak, in rocks, they can develop regular crystal faces on all sides (gypsum crystals in clays, for example). Normally, this is not the case, however; usually the **crystals are attached**; that is, at one end they are intergrown with the subsoil. Naturally, with these crystals only a portion of the faces that are part of the complete crystal form is developed.
- **Skeletal crystals** or **dendrites** form when the crystal substance is deposited primarily at the corners and edges of a crystal.
- **Aggregates**, in contrast to twinned crystals, are irregular intergrowths of several crystals of the same kind. Aggregates may be fibrous, radiating fibrous, reniform, earthy, foliated or lamellar, sparry, crusty, bladed, or globular. The aggregate form is not always typical of a given mineral

[*]Other classifications exist, e.g., Brian Mason and L.G. Berry describe in *Elements of Mineralogy* (W.H. Freeman, 1968, p. 57) a twin as two or more crystals, which are further classified as simple twins if composed of two parts in related orientation and multiple twins if more than two orientations are present. (Editor's note.)

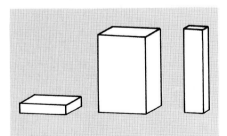

Same form (tetragonal prism with base)—different habit. The crystals are (from left to right) thin tabular, prismatic, acicular.

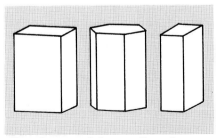

Different form—same habit. Crystal forms shown (from left to right) are: tetragonal prism, hexagonal prism, and rhomboid prism, each with a base.

Form and Habit

Encrustation pseudomorph of marcasite after calcite, Schönbrunn (Vogtland, Germany), crystals over ³/₄ inch (2 cm) in size.

species. Even quite different minerals can appear in the same aggregate form. Goethite, pyrolusite, rockbridgeite, and hematite, for example, can be radiating fibrous with a shallow surface, that is, resembling limonite. Only in exceptional cases is the aggregate form a reliable diagnostic attribute.

- Sometimes minerals occur in crystal forms that belie their internal structure. These are called **pseudomorphs**. They are created when a mineral, while retaining its external form, is replaced by another mineral or is changed into another mineral. Mineralogists speak of pseudomorphs *of* the existing mineral species *after the* previous

Photo: Pseudomorphs can always be recognized by the fact that they possess properties not present in the mineral whose crystal form they display. Calcite, for example, has no metallic luster—although the pseudomorph shown here does.

mineral species. For example, fluorite crystals that have been changed into quartz are called pseudomorphs of quartz after fluorite.

Origin and Mode of Occurrence of Minerals

Although the earth's crust is millions of years old, it continues to be subjected to changes. Some continents rise up above sea level and others are submerged; water and wind erode matter and stratify it again elsewhere. Continuous growth and continuous decay shape our life in the world of nature. Every day, everywhere, crystals grow and minerals form—some relatively quickly, within a few years, others taking centuries to reach any discernible size. Gypsum crystals, for example, can become amazingly large in a relatively short time. This is most apparent in the brine conduits through which the halite (rock salt) dissolved in water is pumped out of mines. Within a few years these conduits are clogged by gypsum crystals. Copper, iron, and zinc sulfates can arise just as swiftly on the walls of mine tunnels. That is the exception, however: Normally a mineral is formed over periods of many thousands or hundreds of thousands of years.

How Do Minerals Form?

Minerals can develop from a solution, from vapor, or from a molten mass (melt), as well as through alteration of already existing minerals in a solid state. The formation of a mineral may be caused by the supersaturation of a solution or a vapor. Tiny crystal nuclei develop, on which additional molecules —depending on the crystal structure in question—can be deposited. Formation from a molten mass, a magma, occurs in a similar manner during the cooling process. When pressure and temperature conditions change, minerals that already have come into existence can alter again.

They adapt, as it were, to the new conditions. Thus hexagonal high-temperature quartz (high quartz) is formed at high temperatures. If the mineral is cooled to a temperature below 1063°F (573°C), trigonal low-temperature quartz (low quartz) is created.

The alteration does not have to be sudden, as with quartz. If the energy required for alteration is not supplied, the change may not occur at all. Diamond, for example, was created under high pressure and at a high temperature, but at normal atmospheric pressure and normal atmospheric temperatures it does not alter. Actually, graphite ought to be produced from it, but—luckily for all owners of diamond jewelry—that does not happen, at least not within a time span that humans can grasp. Experts say that diamond is metastable.

Paragenesis

All the complicated chemical and physical processes that lead to the formation or alteration of a mineral usually do not result in the creation of a sole mineral species; often several mineral species form in the same place. This joint occurrence of minerals is termed paragenesis. We distinguish between frequent (galena and sphalerite), rare (rock crystal, anatase, and wulfenite), and impossible parageneses. The simultaneous

Photo: Blue cavansite crystals on a ▶
mat of stilbite, from the gigantic
basalt quarries near Poona, a large
city in India. 8x

Galena crystals, Freiberg (Germany), 4x

occurrence of minerals of completely different kinds of origins is virtually impossible. For example, kyanite arises at very high pressure, while halite develops through the evaporation of sea water. Their joint appearance is thus almost out of the question. Because the paragenesis can be characteristic of a mineral, it serves as a valuable diagnostic aid, together with the physical and chemical properties.

Where Do Minerals Occur?

To those who collect minerals, it is particularly interesting to know where minerals occur and where they may perhaps be found. For collectors, therefore, some knowledge of mineral deposits is absolutely indispensable. The easiest way to give a good general idea is to divide the occurrences into three main groups, or successions: The igneous succession, the sedimentary succession, and the metamorphic succession.

Photo: A typical paragenesis. Silver-gray galena crystals with tiny reddish brown crystals of sphalerite.

Igneous Succession

This category contains all mineral formations that arose from a molten mass, from gases, or from solutions.

Intramagmatic Deposits

Within bodies of basic plutonic rock, especially in their deepest part, are found beds and strata of chromite and magnetite. As the molten rock cooled, crystals of chromite and magnetite developed first. Because they were heavier than the remaining, still liquid, rock, they sank downward and collected there.

The origin of these deposits can best be explained as follows: If you try to mix oil and water, you will find that it is impossible, because after a short time the

Minerals from Molten Materials

two liquids will separate again. The deposits described above came into existence in exactly the same way. The oxides or sulfides present in the molten rock were so abundant that the melt separated into molten silicate (from which the rock then formed) and molten ore (from which the ore bodies then formed).

One example of such a deposit is the Bushveld complex in the Transvaal province of South Africa. Another type of intramagmatic deposits is found in Canada, in Sudbury, Ontario, where large sulfide ore bodies, some of them almost pure, are mined. They consist primarily of pyrrhotite and pentlandite, an iron-nickel sulfide. They form lens-shaped (lenticular) to vein-shaped beds inside igneous rocks (gabbros and norites). Oxides (like ilmenite and magnetite) can also appear in quite a similar manner.

Pegmatites

In regions that are composed of plutonic rocks, especially granites, are almost always found veins and lenticular bodies—often quite substantial in size—that consist of particularly large-grained

rock. Grain sizes of 4 inches (10 cm) and more are no rarity, and individual crystals can even reach several feet in size. The main components of these rocks—the so-called pegmatites—are, as in the case of the granites, primarily feldspar, quartz, and mica. Very rarely other minerals are also present. In addition, pegmatites often contain a large number of rare minerals that are embedded in large crystals in the rock, including monazite, beryl, topaz, tourmaline, and columbite.

In druses and cavities within the pegmatites are also found beautiful attached crystals of the embedded minerals, which often are of gem quality.

From pegmatites we obtain feldspar and quartz for use in the manufacture of porcelain; beryl, a source of beryllium ore; muscovite, for electrical and heat insulation; and lithium minerals that yield an ore of lithium.

Pegmatites are found in the final phase of the crystallization of plutonic rocks, and in this process some portion of highly volatile components (substances readily converted to the gaseous phase)

Photo: A typical pegmatite specimen: Reddish rose quartz, intergrown with feldspar and a small amount of mica, from Drachselsried in the Bavarian Forest (Germany). Specimen size, about 12 inches (30 cm).

—principally water—is left over. In these residual components are contained all the elements whose atoms are either too large or too small to be incorporated in the normal rock minerals (quartz, feldspar, mica). These are chiefly elements like lithium, beryllium, niobium, tantalum, cesium, and rare earths. These volatile components are highly mobile; lining fissures and cracks they can penetrate deep into the strata, or surrounding rock, and form pegmatites there.

Pegmatites are found in central California, New Mexico, and Utah in the U.S., and in Hagendorf and Pleystein in the Upper Palatinate (northeastern Bavaria) and on the Hühnerkobel in the Bavarian Forest.

Pneumatolytic Deposits

In the strata surrounding granites, often in the granite itself, special mineral formations—called greisen by old miners —are found in veins, along cracks. They are characterized by the fact that, in contrast to the surrounding rock, feldspars are absent, while topaz, lithium-bearing micas, fluorite, and tourmaline are

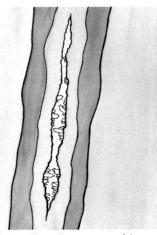

Hydrothermal vein with zonal arrangement of the various minerals and druse cavities.

present in abundance. In rare instances the entire uppermost portion of a granite mass may display these characteristics.

Greisen often contain a great many minerals that are typical of pneumatolytic deposits, including cassiterite, wolframite, zinnwaldite, and apatite.

At the contact zone between molten rock and the surrounding rock (limestone in particular) there are deposits in which the country rock has been altered. It now consists of ore minerals such as pyrite, magnetite, and hematite as well as silicates like hedenbergite, ilvaite, and garnet. Such rocks are also called skarn. All these deposits were created by the action of gases on the surrounding rock. The gases escaped when the molten rock cooled, just as carbon dioxide escapes when a bottle of soda is opened. These gases can migrate a long distance, penetrate the surrounding rock, and alter it substantially. If the gases contained a great deal of hydrofluoric acid, the feldspars of the rock were destroyed, and topaz and fluorite formed, as well as cassiterite, wolframite, and other minerals. The pneumatolytic tin-wolframite deposits originated in this way. If the gases, on the other hand, had a high iron content, they were able to form iron minerals at the place of contact with the surrounding rock; skarn or contact metamorphic deposits were produced.

Fluorite deposits are to be found, for example, at Rosiclare, Hardin Co., Illinois and Marion, Crittenden Co., Kentucky, as well as Altenberg in Saxony (Germany), and Zinnwald in Bohemia (Czech Republic). Topaz crystals exist near Conway, Carrol Co., New Hampshire, in the Pikes Peak area of Colorado, and also in Utah and California.

Typical skarn deposits have been found in the Adirondacks (New York), Utah, and southeast Pennsylvania. In Europe the best places are in Traversella in the Piedmont region (Italy) and in

Hot Solutions

Hydrothermal vein, Freiberg (Germany), about 12 inches (30 cm) wide.

Auerbach on the German Bergstrasse (without ores).

Hydrothermal Veins

If fissures and cracks in the rock become completely filled with mineral formations, veins are created. Replacements result if existing rocks are replaced by subsequently formed minerals; impregnations result if the cavities in porous rocks are filled at a later stage.

The veins often are not uniform in structure: From the selvage (the face that contacts the surrounding rock) inward are found regions with different minerals. Frequently the veins also contain open fissures or cavities in which crystals can grow freely.

All the minerals in hydrothermal veins developed from more or less hot solutions (ranging from 932°F [500°C] and more to lukewarm), hence the term hydrothermal. Well-known hydrothermal veins are located in the desert areas of California and Nevada.

Photo: A hydrothermal vein filled with galena and sphalerite. Clearly visible on both sides is the surrounding rock, which, with the selvage, borders on the vein.

Hydrothermal veins are subdivided as follows:

- High-temperature gold-quartz veins with gold, pyrite, arsenopyrite, chalcopyrite, and quartz. Examples: Nevada Co., California; San Juan Co., Colorado; the Mexican states of Chihuahua, Hidalgo, and Sonora; Brandholz in the Fichtelgebirge (Germany); and in the Hohe Tauern section of the Central Alps (at Rauris and Gastein) in Austria.
- High-temperature pyrite deposits are veins and replacements with pyrite and chalcopyrite, in addition to quartz as a gangue mineral (associated mineral). Examples: Gavorrano (Tuscany, Italy) and Río Tinto (Spain).
- Copper-arsenic deposits with enargite,

Learning About Minerals

chalcocite, and tetrahedrite. Examples: Butte, Montana, and Tsumeb in the Otavi mountain region of Namibia.

- Lead-zinc veins with galena, sphalerite, siderite, tetrahedrite, and chalcopyrite. Examples: Bad Grund in the Harz Mountains (Germany) and Friedrichssegen Mine near Bad Ems (Germany).
- Replacements and impregnations in limestones, some of sedimentary origin, with galena, sphalerite, pyrite, and marcasite. Examples: Bleiberg in Carinthia, Austria and Wiesloch near Heidelberg, Germany.
- Bismuth-cobalt-nickel-silver-uranium formation with cobalt ores and nickel ores, uraninite, and silver minerals. Examples: Wittichen in the Black Forest and Schneeberg in Saxony (both in Germany).
- Hydrothermal veins and replacements without significant quantities of sulfides: quartz veins, barite veins, siderite veins, fluorite veins, and magnesite replacements.
- Lateral secretionary fissure and cavity formations are minerals whose substance derives directly from the surrounding rock; that is, their constituents were merely dissolved, then immediately redeposited in the cavity.
- Cavities or vugs of the Alpine type are a special case: The layering or bedding of the rock is always vertical. This gives rise to an inward pinching of the rock, and this inward deflection is used by the *Strahler* (name given to mountaineers in remote Alpine areas who collect crystals) to detect the presence of a vug. These Alpine cavities contain splendid specimens, some of them considerably large, of rock crystal, smoky quartz, titanite, hematite, anatase, and brookite.

Volcanic Venting
In regions with volcanic activity, volcanic gases often issue around active as well as extinct volcanoes. At these vents or fissures, crusts and crystals of minerals are formed from the gases. These minerals include sulfur, sal ammoniac, and alum.

Occurrences of this type include the solfataras at Vulcano Island and at Pozzuoli (near Naples, Italy).

Subvolcanic Formations
Volcanic rocks that have solidified just below the earth's surface often contain deposits of minerals formed at high temperatures, such as huebnerite, together with minerals formed at low temperatures, such as rhodochrosite. This category also includes the gold-silver deposits that contain abundant quantities of tellurides, such as nagyagite and sylvanite.

Examples of such formations are the gold deposits in Transylvania (Romania) and at Cripple Creek, Colorado.

Submarine Vented Deposits
When volcanic gases issue from the ocean floor, large, stratified deposits of iron containing hematite and pyrite are frequently created.

One example is the iron deposits of the

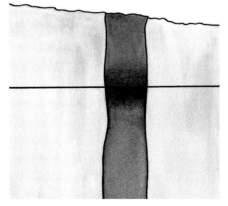

Hydrothermal vein with oxidation zone (top), cementation zone in the area of the groundwater table (solid line), and unaltered vein (bottom).

Mineral Formation by Weathering

Titanite, Habachtal (Austria), 10x

Lahn-Dill Basin (Germany), which arose in the Paleozoic era when this region was an ocean floor.

Sedimentary Succession
This category includes all mineral formations that came into being at the earth's surface by oxidation, weathering, erosion, and deposition (sedimentation).

Kaolinite and Bauxite Deposits
Granitic rocks weather at the earth's surface. During this process, feldspars alter into clay minerals, particularly kaolinite. Often the structure of the rock is preserved in its entirety; it has merely been softened by the clay minerals. In this way, large kaolinite deposits can form,

Photo: A characteristic specimen from an Alpine cavity. Typical tabular titanite crystals—known as sphene—are attached to a mat of tiny pericline crystals.

and they are quarried for the purpose of producing porcelain. In the weathering of rocks with a high aluminum content, bauxites are formed, and they serve as raw materials for the production of aluminum.

Kaolinite deposits of this kind exist, for example, in Pennsylvania, Virginia, Georgia, Illinois, and South Carolina.

Limonite, Siegerland (Germany), 5x

Oxidation and Cementation Zones

Wherever a deposit, a vein, extends all the way to the earth's surface (miners say the vein forms an "outcrop"), its appearance and its mineral content are changed substantially: The vein no longer contains any pyritiferous ores, and the most common mineral is limonite. Intergrown with it or attached in its cavities are found oxidation minerals such as malachite, azurite, cerussite, and wulfenite. This zone, the oxidation zone or "iron hat"—as miners call it because of the dominance of limonite—has a lower metal content than the unaltered, non-oxidized deposit at greater depths.

Approximately at the level of the groundwater table, between the oxidation

Photo: Limonite, a conglomerate of goethite with amorphous iron hydroxides, is the typical mineral of the oxidation zone.

zone and the unaltered deposit, lies an area with metal-rich minerals such as chalcocite, native copper, cuprite, argentite, and native silver. The zone that has a higher metal content than the unaltered deposit is known as the cementation zone. The alteration of this deposit from the top downward occurred as follows: At the earth's surface the minerals come in contact with water containing carbon dioxide, and they weather. During that process the bulk of the metallic content is

From Streams and Rivers

dissolved and vanishes, along with the water, into the depths. Left behind are iron oxides and iron hydroxides, mainly limonite. At the level of the groundwater table the water, charged with metal ions, comes in contact with unaltered sulfides. They cause the more precious metals to be displaced from the solution and be precipitated out through contact with the sulfides of the less-precious metals (iron). Thus it happens that the cementation zone contains many minerals of the more-precious metals, such as copper, silver, and gold.

Placer Deposits

We all know that gold sometimes can be washed out of the sand in stream and river beds. It is less well known that other minerals also can be found there. These are primarily minerals distinguished by their high specific gravity and their chemical resistance, such as platinum, garnet, ilmenite, rutile, and monazite.

Such deposits—known as placer or alluvial ore deposits—originate when minerals are exposed during the weather-ing of rocks or deposits and are carried off with the water. Because they are heavier than other minerals, they become particularly concentrated at some spots in the bodies of water—for example, in rivers or streams below a waterfall, or where the water current abruptly slack-ens. Heavy minerals also can become concentrated on the beach or in the surf zone (beach or surf placers).

Placers may have originated even millions of years ago. Well known is the Witwatersrand Conglomerate (South Africa), which is a fossilized placer dating from prehistoric times. In addition to gold, it also contains detrital uraninite and pyrite. The presence of those two miner-als, which today are not stable in placers because they are oxidized immediately by the atmospheric oxygen, suggests that at

Photos: Carbonates (cerussite, for example), sulfates, phosphates, and arsenates form in the oxidation zone, while in the cementation zone primarily sulfides rich in precious metals (such as stephanite and argentite) occur.

Cerussite, Siegerland (Germany), 4x

Stephanite, Freiberg (Germany), 3x

Learning About Minerals

minerals by metamorphic processes—that is, changes in pressure or temperature, or both.

Alteration of Existing Minerals
In nature, no deposits are produced by metamorphic processes. However, the mineral content of already existing deposits is altered by metamorphism. Thus magnetite can be produced from a great variety of iron deposits through metamorphism. During the course of this process, new minerals form in the rocks, then these minerals conform to the changed pressure and heat conditions and become stable.

the time the Witwatersrand Conglomerate formed there was practically no oxygen available in the atmosphere.

Saline Deposits
Enormous beds of salts were created by the evaporation of sea water. When they were covered over by layers impermeable to water, such as clay or gypsum, they were preserved. The deposits from which we now get the majority of our rock salt and potassium salt came into existence in that way.

In saline lakes in arid regions, large layers of borates like colemanite, ulexite, and borax were deposited in the same fashion. Exceptionally large deposits of this type are located in the western United States, particularly in California and Utah—for example, Searles Lake or the Great Salt Lake.

Metamorphic Succession
The metamorphic succession includes all mineral formations created from other

Mineral Deposits and Their Characteristic Minerals
In the following table the most important minerals are arranged according to the type of deposit in which they occur. They are typical of metamorphically altered deposits, but are also found in others. Quartz, for example, is a thoroughly characteristic mineral for certain types of deposits, such as hydrothermal veins or Alpine cavities, but it also appears in almost all other types of deposits, though often in a minor role. However, it is equally likely to be absent on occasion in a type of deposit where quartz is typically present. There are, though rarely, hydrothermal veins that bear no quartz. On the other hand, there are also minerals whose appearance is confined to only one of the types of deposits listed.

Mineral Deposits

Igneous Succession

Intramagmatic deposits	Chromite, magnetite, pyrrhotite, pentlandite
Pegmatites	Beryl, tourmaline, spodumene, amblygonite, columbite
Pneumatolytic deposits	Topaz, zinnwaldite, fluorite, apatite, cassiterite, wolframite, scheelite, arsenopyrite, stannite
Hydrothermal veins High-temperature gold-quartz veins	Quartz, native gold, arsenopyrite, pyrite, tourmaline, scheelite
High-temperature pyrite deposits	Quartz, pyrite, chalcopyrite
Copper-arsenic deposits Lead-zinc veins	Chalcocite, bornite, enargite, tennantite, galena, sphalerite, chalcopyrite, pyrite, siderite, calcite
Replacements and impregnations in limestones	Galena, sphalerite, pyrite, barite, calcite, dolomite
Bismuth-cobalt-nickel-silver-uranium formation	Native bismuth, chloanthite, skutterudite, argentite, proustite, pyrargyrite, uraninite
Hydrothermal veins with relatively small amounts of sulfides	Quartz, hematite, siderite, rhodochrosite
Fissure and cavity formations	Rock crystal, smoky quartz, titanite, anatase, rutile
Products of volcanic venting	Sulfur, alum, salmiak
Subvolcanic formations	Huebnerite, enargite, rhodochrosite, nagyagite, sylvanite, gold
Submarine vented deposits	Hematite, magnetite, quartz

Sedimentary Succession

Kaolinite and bauxite deposits	Kaolinite, diaspore, boehmite
Oxidation and cementation zones	Limonite, malachite, azurite, cerussite, anglesite, wulfenite, cuprite, covellite, chalcocite, native copper
Placer deposits	Gold, platinum, diamond, garnet, monazite, zircon, ilmenite, corundum
Saline deposits	Halite, sylvite, anhydrite, gypsum

Metamorphic Succession

Alterations of existing minerals	Magnetite, cordierite, pyrrhotite, garnet

Gemstones

Minerals that are noteworthy for their special durability, rarity, and beauty —such as diamonds, rubies, sapphires, emeralds, and topazes—are called gemstones, or precious stones. Along with the so-called semiprecious stones, which are less hard and less scarce, they are used in making jewelry. The precious stone and semiprecious stone concepts are impossible to define unambiguously. Because the terms are applied in very different ways, however, differentiating between them is actually not necessary.

Identifying gems, or cut precious stones, is a great deal more difficult than identifying unprocessed minerals, as some portion of the distinguishing characteristics vanishes during the cutting process (for example, the crystal form and the associated minerals). Other properties, such as hardness, cleavage, and tenacity, cannot be tested because the stone would have to be damaged.

Identification of cut precious stones relies principally on optical properties, such as refraction of light, or on examination under a microscope—the study of the inclusions, for example.

Over time an entire branch of science —gemology—has developed. Because the emphasis of this book is on the identification of minerals, only the most important types of cuts are presented here, for the sake of completeness.

Types of Cuts

Transparent gemstones are often cut into facets, so that their surface consists of a great many small planar surfaces, through which the incident ray of light is refracted many times. This increases the brilliance of the stone.

Among the facets, the **brilliant cut** is quite popular. It is used most often for diamonds, but is in common use for many other transparent gems as well.

For opaque or merely translucent gems, the **cabochon cut** is especially suitable. It results in pieces with a rounded, plain hemispherical surface. The base does not have to be circular; rather, it is adapted to the natural, given conditions of the stone. With this type of cut, the asterism is displayed to excellent advantage. Asterism is an optical phenomenon based on the fact that in many minerals, extremely small fibers of another mineral are embedded. If you illuminate a cylindrically ground stone of this kind with a point source of light, refraction on the ingrown fibers will result in the appearance of a star. Asterism is most common in rubies, sapphires, some pyroxenes, and rose quartz.

In recent years a new group of mineral collectors—people who cut and polish gemstones as a hobby or who collect cut stones—has greatly increased its numbers. These people collect not pieces of jewelry, but unset minerals that they either cut and polished themselves or bought already cut. Because the pieces are not worn as jewelry, such collections may also contain cut minerals that well might be described as gems but are unavailable in the jewelry trade by virtue of their low degree of hardness or their great scarcity. Collectors store their pieces in appropriate display cases.

Precious stones and semiprecious ▶ stones are minerals that are made into jewelry.

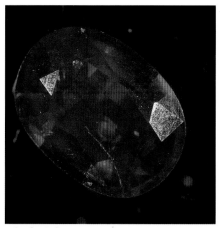
Ruby, faceted

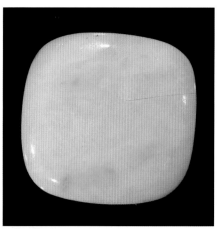
Jade, cabochon

Lazurite, cabochon

Yellow sapphire, cabochon

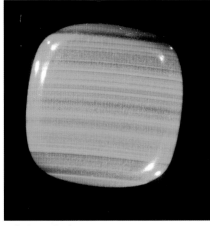
Malachite, cabochon

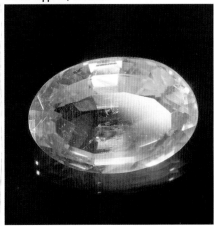
Aquamarine, faceted

Globular reniform sphalerite from Wiesloch (Baden, Germany). Over 3 inches (8 cm) wide. In cross section such aggregates reveal attractive concentric bandings, light brown to dark brown in color.

Identifying Minerals

On the following pages you will find the identification section of this nature guide. There the most important minerals, along with all their properties, are described in detail and arranged according to streak and hardness, indicated by Barron's system of color coding. To make the crystal shapes easier to recognize, we have included numerous sketches of crystals, computer-calculated and drawn especially for this nature guide.

Advice and Tips on Identification

Using Barron's Color Key as an Aid to Identification

The minerals in this section are divided into seven color groups in accordance with the color of their streak.

Blue bar:
On pages 50 to 55 you will find the minerals that have a light blue to greenish blue streak.

Red bar:
On pages 56 to 63 you will find the minerals that have a rose-pink to brownish red streak.

Yellow bar:
On pages 64 to 71 you will find the minerals that have a light yellow to orange streak.

Brown bar:
On pages 72 to 85 you will

find the minerals that have a yellowish brown to reddish brown streak.

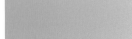

Green bar:
On pages 86 to 103 you will find the minerals that have a light green, bluish green, grayish green to dark green streak.

Black bar:
On pages 104 to 135 you will find the minerals that have a gray to black streak.

White bar:
On pages 136 to 211 you will find the minerals that have a white or extremely pale streak, as well as all the minerals that are harder than the streak plate material.

The Degree of Hardness

Along with the colored bars, you will find data on the hardness of the minerals. Within the individual streak-color groups the minerals are arranged in order of increasing hardness.

How to Identify a Mineral

To identify a mineral, you have to test all the properties listed in the profiles, in the following order:
- Streak
- Hardness/tenacity
- Density
- Color of mineral/luster
- Cleavage/fracture
- Crystal form

In the chapter Learning About Minerals you will learn exactly what you need to look for when testing these properties.

In the profiles, additional determinative features, including the type of occurrence, associated minerals, and special properties (e.g., fluorescence, solubility) will give you additional pointers.

Similar Minerals tells you what properties distinguish the minerals that are easily mistaken for others.

About the Identification Section

Species Chosen for Inclusion

In this book you will find the most important species of minerals.

Naturally such a selection is always somewhat arbitrary, and some collectors may possibly look in vain for their favorite rare mineral.

For this guide I chose minerals that occur with frequency, that possess some economic importance (for example, as raw materials of metals), and that are especially popular with collectors and well represented in their collections.

The Profiles

All the color photos show the individual minerals in characteristic form. Minerals can possess a great diversity of forms; each mineral specimen is almost unique. Nevertheless, to show the multiplicity of developments or colors of some minerals, several characteristic developments have been depicted, wherever possible.

The **descriptions** contain all important data necessary for identification of the minerals by external distinguishing features. These data are presented concisely and accurately.

Mineral names: In each case the mineral name given is the international term designated by the Commission on Mineral Names of the International Mineralogical Association, taken here as the highest authority. Also given, when applicable, are alternative international names (listed first) and English common names.

The Crystal Drawings

In the case of the minerals that appear more commonly in well-developed crystals, drawings of the typical crystal outlines most usual for this mineral form are also supplied.

These sketches were newly calculated and drawn especially for this book with the help of a special computer program, to guarantee exact representation that is in accordance with the latest scientific findings. If no crystal drawings are present, the mineral as a rule does not occur in well-developed crystals.

Photo Captions

The caption accompanying each photo lists the mineral species, the origin of the mineral, and the photo enlargement. Most of the minerals are shown magnified (for example, 5x), a few are shown smaller than they are in reality (for example, 0.5×).

Abbreviations

inch (cm) indicates size in the captions

x indicates enlargement in the captions and text

Blue

The following pages describe minerals that have a light blue, blue, or greenish blue streak. All these minerals are monochromatic; that is, their body color is also more or less blue.

Numerous other minerals that are blue in color, but have a white streak, are grouped together with the other minerals possessing a white streak.

Azurite crystal from Tsumeb (Namibia). Crystal size is over 1 inch (3 cm).

Blue Streak

2 Liroconite, Cornwall (England), 3x

3 Linarite, Cornwall (England), 3x

Natural crystals of chalcanthite are extremely rare, but easy to synthesize. Watch out! Almost all the crystal specimens available for sale are fakes.

1 Chalcanthite, Arkansas, 5x

1 Chalcanthite

Hardness: $2\frac{1}{2}$.
Density: 2.2–2.3.
Streak: Blue.
Chemical Formula: $CuSO_4 \cdot 5H_2O$
Color: Blue; vitreous luster.
Cleavage: Scarcely discernible; fracture conchoidal.
Tenacity: Brittle.
Crystal Form: Triclinic; rarely prismatic, lens-shaped, stalactitic, crusty, massive.
Occurrence: In the oxidation zone.
Associated Minerals: Chalcopyrite, malachite, brochantite.
Special Property: Water soluble.
Similar Minerals: Azurite is darker blue and not water soluble.

2 Liroconite
Hardness: $2-2\frac{1}{2}$.
Density: 2.95.
Streak: Blue to bluish green.
Chemical Formula: $Cu_2Al(AsO_4)(OH)_4 \cdot 4H_2O$
Color: Blue to bluish green; vitreous luster.
Cleavage: Poor; fracture conchoidal.
Tenacity: Brittle.
Crystal Form: Monoclinic; lens-shaped, as crusts.
Occurrence: In the oxidation zone.
Associated Minerals: Clinoclase, azurite, malachite.
Similar Minerals: Azurite and malachite are a different color, and they effervesce with hydrochloric acid.

3/4 Linarite
Hardness: $2\frac{1}{2}$.
Density: 5.3–5.5.
Streak: Light blue.
Chemical Formula: $PbCu[(OH)_2/SO_4]$
Color: Blue; vitreous luster.
Cleavage: Distinct, but discernible only in relatively large crystals. Fracture

4 Linarite, Blanchard Mine (USA), 8x

5 Caledonite, Scotland, 10x

6 Boleite, Boleo (Mexico), 8x

conchoidal.
Tenacity: Brittle.
Crystal Form: Monoclinic; prismatic to, more rarely, tabular, often with numerous faces, crusty, earthy.
Occurrence: In the oxidation zone.
Associated Minerals: Galena, chalcopyrite, brochantite, malachite, cerussite.
Similar Minerals: Azurite effervesces with hydrochloric acid.

5 Caledonite
Hardness: 2$^1/_2$–3.
Density: 5.6.
Streak: Whitish blue.
Chemical Formula: $Cu_2Pb_5(SO_4)CO_3(OH)_6$
Color: Blue, bluish green; vitreous luster.
Cleavage: Perfect; fracture uneven.
Tenacity: Brittle.
Crystal Form: Orthorhombic; prismatic, acicular.
Occurrence: In the oxidation zone.
Associated Minerals: Leadhillite, anglesite.
Similar Minerals: Linarite has a different crystal form.

6 Boleite
Hardness: 3–3$^1/_2$.
Density: 5.10.
Streak: Blue.
Chemical Formula: $Pb_9Cu_8Ag_3Cl_{21}(OH)_{16} \cdot H_2O$
Color: Blue; vitreous luster.
Cleavage: Perfect; fracture conchoidal.
Tenacity: Brittle.
Crystal Form: Tetragonal; pseudo-octahedral and pseudocubic.
Occurrence: Oxidation zone.
Associated Minerals: Laurionite, cumengeite.
Similar Minerals: Diaboleite and cumengeite have a different crystal form.

2 Cyanotrichite, France, 6x

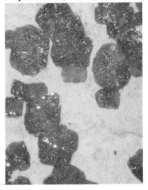

3 Cornetite, Shaba (Zaire), 4x

1 Connellite, Cornwall (England), 6x

1 Connellite
Hardness: 3.
Density: 3.41.
Streak: Blue.
Chemical Formula:
$Cu_{19}Cl_2SO_4(OH)_{32} \cdot H_2O$
Color: Blue; vitreous luster.
Cleavage: Not discernible;
fracture conchoidal.
Tenacity: Brittle.
Crystal Form: Orthorhom-
bic; acicular, often intergrown
in tufts.
Occurrence: Oxidation zone.
Associated Minerals:
Azurite, malachite.
Similar Minerals:
Cyanotrichite is lighter blue.

2 Cyanotrichite
Hardness: $3^1/_2$–4.
Density: 3.7–3.9.
Streak: Blue.
Chemical Formula:
$Cu_4Al_2[(OH)_{12}/SO_4] \cdot 2H_2O$
Color: Sky-blue; silky to
vitreous luster.
Cleavage: None; fracture
uneven.
Tenacity: Brittle.
Crystal Form: Orthorhom-
bic; acicular to elongated
tabular, capillary, in tufts.
Occurrence: Oxidation zone.
Associated Minerals:
Brochantite, smithsonite,
malachite, azurite.
Similar Minerals: Azurite is

much darker.

3 Cornetite
Hardness: $4^1/_2$.
Density: 4.10.
Streak: Blue.
Chemical Formula:
$Cu_3PO_4(OH)_3$
Color: Greenish blue to dark
blue; vitreous luster.
Cleavage: None; fracture
uneven.
Tenacity: Brittle.
Crystal Form: Orthorhom-
bic; short prismatic, often
rounded; radiating fibrous.
Occurrence: Oxidation zone.
Associated Minerals:
Malachite, pseudomalachite,

4 Azurite, La Sal (Utah), 2x

5 Azurite, Brixlegg (Tyrol, Austria), 3x

6 Lazurite, Afghanistan, 4x

brochantite.
Similar Minerals: Azurite and clinoclase are a different color. Linarite occurs in a different paragenesis.

4/5 Azurite
(Azure copper ore, Chessylite)
Hardness: 3¹/₂–4.
Density: 3.7–3.9.
Streak: Blue.
Chemical Formula:
$Cu_3[OH/CO_3]_2$
Color: Deep blue; vitreous luster.
Cleavage: Perfect; fracture conchoidal.
Tenacity: Brittle.

Crystal Form: Monoclinic; columnar to tabular, globular groups and crusts, radiating fibrous, massive, earthy.
Occurrence: Oxidation zone.
Associated Minerals: Malachite, cuprite.
Special Property: Effervesces with hydrochloric acid.
Similar Minerals: Azurite is distinguished from all other minerals by its color and its ability to effervesce when moistened with HCl.

6 Lazurite
(Lapis lazuli)
Hardness: 5–6.

Density: 2.38–2.42.
Streak: Blue.
Chemical Formula:
$Na_8[S/(AlSiO_4)_6]$
Color: Blue; vitreous luster, greasy luster on fracture surface.
Cleavage: Scarcely discernible; fracture conchoidal.
Tenacity: Brittle.
Crystal Form: Isometric; usually massive, granular, compact.
Occurrence: In marbles with a high sodium content.
Associated Minerals: Diopside, pyrite, calcite.
Similar Minerals: Azurite effervesces with HCl.

Red

Minerals whose streak reveals shades of red, ranging from rose-pink to brownish red, are discussed on the pages that follow.

The transition to the brown streak, however, is not clear-cut, so that in borderline cases you will need to check two categories when trying to make an identification, namely minerals with a red streak and minerals with a brown streak.

Minerals with a red streak are relatively rare. If a streak of this color does turn up, however, these minerals can be identified easily.

Erythrite crystals found at Schneeberg, Saxony (Germany). Size of crystals: over 1 inch (3 cm).

1 Erythrite, Schneeberg (Saxony, Germany), 8x

2 Kermesite, Pezinok (Czechoslovakia), 2x

Pink erythrite is created during the weathering of cobalt ores and, consequently, it is a typical indicator for their presence. Cobalt ores that are only slightly exposed to weathering at the surface become coated at once with a pink crust.

1 Erythrite
(Cobalt bloom)
Hardness: 2.
Density: 3.07.
Streak: Pink.
Chemical Formula:
$Co_3(AsO_4)_2 \cdot 8H_2O$
Color: Red, with a violet cast, pink; vitreous luster, pearly luster on cleavage surfaces.
Cleavage: Perfect; fracture uneven.
Tenacity: Nonbrittle; laminae flexible.
Crystal Form: Monoclinic; acicular to tabular, radiated, earthy, crusty, massive.
Occurrence: In the oxidation zone of cobalt-bearing deposits.
Associated Minerals: Safflorite, cobaltite, skutterudite, native bismuth.
Similar Minerals: The characteristic color of erythrite rules out any misidentification.

2 Kermesite
Hardness: $1-1^1/_2$.
Density: 4.68.
Streak: Brownish red, red.
Chemical Formula: Sb_2S_2O
Color: Red; vitreous to adamantine luster.
Cleavage: Scarcely discernible; fracture fibrous.
Tenacity: Nonbrittle.
Crystal Form: Monoclinic; acicular, capillary, as coating.
Occurrence: In the oxidation zone of antimony deposits.
Associated Minerals: Stibnite.
Similar Minerals: Considering the paragenesis, kermesite cannot be confused with any other mineral.

3 Miargyrite, Romania, 4x

4 Cinnabar, Eisenerz (Austria), 5x

Cinnabar is the most important mercury ore. Even today it continues to be mined in fairly large quantities to obtain this metal. At one time, however, mercury was far more significant than now: It once was used in the extraction of gold by the amalgamation process.

6 Cinnabar, Siegerland (Germany), 8x

3 Miargyrite

Hardness: 2$^{1}/_{2}$.
Density: 5.25.
Streak: Red.
Chemical Formula: AgSbS$_2$
Color: Gray to black; metallic luster.
Cleavage: Not discernible; fracture conchoidal.
Tenacity: Brittle.
Crystal Form: Monoclinic; thick tabular, massive.
Occurrence: In hydrothermal silver-ore veins.
Associated Minerals: Pyrargyrite, argentite.
Similar Minerals: Stephanite and polybasite have a different streak;

proustite and pyrargyrite are a different color.

4/5 Cinnabar
Hardness: 2–2$^{1}/_{2}$.
Density: 8.1.
Streak: Red.
Chemical Formula: HgS
Color: Light red, dark red, brownish red; adamantine luster, in fine granules often dull.
Cleavage: Perfect prismatic; fracture splintery.
Tenacity: Nonbrittle.
Crystal Form: Trigonal; rarely in thick tabular to rhombohedral crystals; usually massive, granular,

earthy, radiated.
Occurrence: In low-temperature hydrothermal veins, in the oxidation zone, at points where volcanic gases issue from the surrounding rocks.
Associated Minerals: Quartz, chalcedony, pyrite.
Similar Minerals: "Ruby jack" sphalerite is much lighter and harder and has a different cleavage. Hematite, cuprite, and rutile are harder.

59

Red Streak

1 Proustite, Schneeberg (Saxony, Germany) 4x

2 Pyrargyrite, Harz (Germany), 4x

3 Pyrargyrite, Harz (Germany), 6x

1 Proustite
(Light ruby silver)
Hardness: 2$^1/_2$.
Density: 5.5–5.7.
Streak: Scarlet red.
Chemical Formula:
Ag_3AsS_3
Color: Scarlet to cinnabar red; adamantine to metallic luster, sometimes with dull tarnish.
Cleavage: Sometimes distinct rhombohedral; fracture conchoidal.
Tenacity: Brittle.
Crystal Form: Trigonal; prismatic to pyramidal, usually attached, often massive.
Occurrence: In subvolcanic gold-silver deposits and hydrothermal veins.
Associated Minerals: Argentite, stephanite, polybasite, native silver.
Similar Minerals: Pyrargyrite is darker and has a darker streak. Cuprite has a different crystal form.

2/3 Pyrargyrite
(Dark ruby silver)
Hardness: 2$^1/_2$–3.
Density: 5.85.
Streak: Cherry-red.
Chemical Formula:
Ag_3SbS_3
Color: Dark red to grayish black, red translucent; metallic luster.
Cleavage: Sometimes distinct; fracture conchoidal.
Tenacity: Brittle.
Crystal Form: Trigonal; pseudorhombohedral and pseudoscalenohedral in appearance, always attached, massive.
Occurrence: In silver ore veins.
Associated Minerals: Proustite, argentite, stephanite, galena, calcite.
Similar Minerals: Proustite is lighter red.

4 Cuprite, Siegerland (Germany), 6x

5 Cuprite, Siegerland (Germany), 6x

6 Copper, Siegerland (Germany), 6x

4/5 Cuprite
(Ruby copper)
Hardness: 3¹/₂–4.
Density: 6.15.
Streak: Brownish red.
Chemical Formula: Cu_2O
Color: Deep red to brownish red; metallic luster, adamantine luster, in aggregates also dull.
Cleavage: Discernible octahedral; fracture conchoidal.
Tenacity: Brittle.
Crystal Form: Isometric; octahedrons, more rarely in cubes, elongated capillary crystals (chalcotrichite), granular, massive.
Occurrence: In the oxidation zone of copper deposits.
Associated Minerals: Native copper, malachite, limonite.
Similar Minerals: Hematite is harder; cinnabar has a different crystal form.

6 Copper

Hardness: 2¹/₂–3.
Density: 8.93.
Streak: Copper-red, metallic.
Chemical Formula: Cu
Color: Copper-red; metallic luster.
Cleavage: None; fracture hackly.
Tenacity: Nonbrittle, ductile.
Crystal Form: Isometric; cubes, octahedrons, usually extremely distorted, dendritic, also in sheets and wirelike forms, massive.
Occurrence: In the cementation zone of many copper deposits; in vesicles in volcanic rocks.
Associated Minerals: Malachite, cuprite, calcite.
Similar Minerals: Silver is a different color and has a different streak.

61

1 Crocoite, Callenberg (Saxony, Germany), 8x

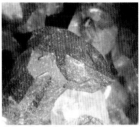

2 Roselite, Schneeberg (Ger.), 10x

3 Lepidocrocite, Siegerland (Germany), 2x

Thin sheets of lepidocrocite show an intense red translucence.

1 Crocoite

Hardness: 2¹/₂–3.
Density: 5.9–6.0
Streak: Orange.
Chemical Formula: $PbCrO_4$
Color: Red with occasional yellow cast; greasy to adamantine luster.
Cleavage: Discernible; fracture conchoidal.
Tenacity: Nonbrittle.
Crystal Form: Monoclinic; acicular to prismatic, tabular, massive, as film.
Occurrence: In the oxidation zone of lead deposits when in contact with chromium-bearing weathering solutions.
Associated Minerals: Cerussite, pyromorphite.
Similar Minerals: Cinnabar has a different crystal form; realgar is distinguished by its paragenesis. Cuprite has a different crystal form.

2 Roselite
Hardness: 3¹/₂.
Density: 3.50–3.74.
Streak: Reddish.
Chemical Formula: $Ca_2(Co,Mg)(AsO_4)_2 \cdot 2H_2O$
Color: Dark pink; vitreous luster.
Cleavage: Perfect; fracture uneven.
Tenacity: Brittle.
Crystal Form: Monoclinic; in thick tabular crystals, massive crusts.
Occurrence: In the oxidation zone.
Associated Minerals: Erythrite.
Similar Minerals: Roselite has a very distinctive crystal form.

3 Lepidocrocite
Hardness: 5.
Density: 4.0.
Streak: Reddish.
Chemical Formula: FeOOH
Color: Ruby-red to yellowish red; adamantine luster.
Cleavage: Perfect; fracture uneven.

4 Hematite, Cumberland (Eng.), 0.2x

5 Hematite, Zillertal (Austria), 0.2x

Compact hematite is also known as "bloodstone" because it "bleeds": When it is cut, its powder turns the abrasion liquid red.

6 Hematite, Siegerland (Germany), 4x

Tenacity: Brittle.
Crystal Form:
Orthorhombic; tabular, radiated, lamellar, massive.
Occurrence: In the oxidation zone.
Associated Minerals:
Goethite, pyrolusite.
Similar Minerals: The red color and streak distinguish lepidocrocite from goethite. Hematite is harder.

4/5/6 Hematite
Hardness: 6¹/₂.
Density: 5.2–5.3.
Streak: Red to reddish brown, black if titanium content is low.
Chemical Formula: Fe_2O_3
Color: Massive aggregates and thin flat scales red, otherwise metallic blackish-gray, often tarnished iridescent; metallic luster to dull.
Cleavage: None, often partings; fracture conchoidal.
Tenacity: Brittle.
Crystal Form: Trigonal; bipyramidal, thick to thin tabular, rosette-shaped ("iron roses"), often massive, foliat-

ed, radiating fibrous, also with smooth surface ("kidney ore"), earthy, crusty.
Occurrence: Microscopic in almost all rocks, especially metamorphic rock; in pneumatolytic and hydrothermal veins, at points where volcanic gases issue, in contact metasomatic deposits.
Associated Minerals:
Magnesite, pyrite.
Similar Minerals: Magnesite and ilmenite have a black streak; cuprite, cinnabar, and realgar are softer.

63

Yellow

Minerals with a yellow, orange to yellowish-ocher streak are discussed on the pages that follow.

One particularly noteworthy mineral with a yellow streak is native gold, whose golden-yellow streak also has a metallic brightness.

Tabular uranocircite crystals, some over $3/4$ inch (1 cm) in size, from Bergen (Vogtland, Germany).

1 Realgar, China, 2x

2 Realgar, China, 4x

3 Orpiment, Peru, 6x

1/2 Realgar

Hardness: 1¹/₂.
Density: 3.5–3.6.
Streak: Orangish yellow.
Chemical Formula: AsS
Color: Deep red to orange, translucent to opaque; adamantine to greasy luster.
Cleavage: Scarcely discernible; fracture conchoidal.
Tenacity: Thin scales flexible, nonbrittle.
Crystal Form: Monoclinic; prismatic, acicular, powdery, massive.
Occurrence: In ore veins formed at low temperatures, as a deposit from hot springs and volcanic gases, on clays and limestones, as a weathering residue of arsenic-containing ores.
Associated Minerals: Orpiment, stibnite.
Special Property: On exposure to light slowly disintegrates to an orange-yellow powder of the same composition, hence protect from light.
Similar Minerals: Cuprite has a different crystal form and streak. Cinnabar is much heavier and has perfect cleavage.

3 Orpiment

Hardness: 1¹/₂–2.
Density: 3.48.
Streak: Light yellow.
Chemical Formula: As_2S_3
Color: Lemon-yellow to orange-yellow; greasy luster.
Cleavage: Highly perfect; fracture micaceous.
Tenacity: Nonbrittle, sectile, cleavage laminae flexible but inelastic.
Crystal Form: Monoclinic; lenticular, radiating fibrous, foliated, radiated, massive.
Occurrence: In hydrothermal veins and argillaceous rocks.

Yellow Streak

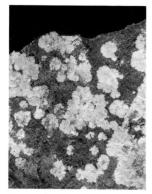

4 Uranophane, Bergen (Ger.), 8x

Danger! All uranium minerals are radioactive and therefore injurious to your health. When handling uranium minerals, never eat, smoke, or drink, and be sure to wash your hands well afterward. Always keep these minerals out of children's reach, and never store them in rooms that are lived in.

5 Uranocircite, Bergen (Vogtland, Germany), 4x

Associated Minerals: Realgar, arsenic minerals.
Similar Minerals: Greenockite has a different crystal form; its paragenesis with sphalerite is characteristic.

4 Uranophane
(Uranotile)
Hardness: 2¹/₂.
Density: 3.9.
Streak: Light yellow.
Chemical Formula: $CaH_2[UO_2/SiO_4]_2 \cdot 5H_2O$
Color: Straw-yellow to deep yellow; vitreous luster.
Cleavage: Not discernible; fracture conchoidal.

Tenacity: Brittle.
Crystal Form: Monoclinic; acicular to capillary, in tufts, radiated, massive, earthy.
Occurrence: In the oxidation zone of uranium deposits.
Associated Minerals: Autunite, torbernite, zeunerite.
Similar Minerals: Strunzite and cacoxenite appear in altogether different parageneses.

5 Uranocircite
Hardness: 2¹/₂.
Density: 3.5.
Streak: Yellowish.
Chemical Formula: $Ba[UO_2/PO_4]_2 \cdot 8H_2O$
Color: Yellow with green

cast; vitreous luster, on cleavage surfaces pearly luster.
Cleavage: Perfect basal; fracture uneven.
Tenacity: Brittle to nonbrittle.
Crystal Form: Tetragonal; tabular.
Occurrence: In the oxidation zone.
Associated Minerals: Torbernite, autunite.
Special Property: Fluoresces in UV light.
Similar Minerals: Torbernite is green and not fluorescent. Autunite often is indistinguishable by ordinary methods.

1 Gold, Michigan Bluff, California, 5x

2 Gold, Venezuela, 3x

3 Gold, Australia, 1x

Nuggets are roundish, rolled pieces of native gold that can be found in rivers or streams.

1/2/3 Gold
Hardness: 2¹/₂–3.
Density: 15.5–19.3.
Streak: Golden yellow.
Chemical Formula: Au
Color: Golden yellow to brassy yellow; metallic luster.
Cleavage: None; fracture hackly.
Tenacity: Nonbrittle; highly ductile, can be hammered into thin leaves.
Crystal Form: Isometric; octahedrons, cubes, seldom well developed, usually distorted, dendritic, in sheets or wirelike shapes, often massive, embedded, as rounded nuggets.

Occurrence: In high-temperature to moderate-temperature hydrothermal veins, in placers found in rivers and streams.
Associated Minerals: Quartz, arsenopyrite, pyrite, tourmaline.
Similar Minerals: Pyrite, chalcopyrite, and marcasite have a different streak and are not ductile.

4 Cacoxenite
Hardness: 3.
Density: 2.3.
Streak: White to yellowish.
Chemical Formula: $Fe_4[OH/PO_4]_3 \cdot 12H_2O$

Color: Golden-yellow to brownish; silky to vitreous luster.
Cleavage: Not discernible; fracture fibrous.
Tenacity: Brittle.
Crystal Form: Hexagonal; acicular, capillary, usually globular, fibrous, radiating fibrous.
Occurrence: In phosphate pegmatites and limonite deposits.
Associated Minerals: Beraunite, strengite, rockbridgeite.
Similar Minerals: Strunzite is paler yellow.

4 Cacoxenite, Sweden, 6x

5 Beraunite, Cornwall (England), 8x

Phosphate minerals like cacoxenite or beraunite are quite popular with many mineral collectors. Three sources of cacoxenite are Polk County (Arkansas), Antwerp (New York), and Cornwall (England). Good locations for beraunite are Pennington County (South Dakota) and the Palermo Mine in New Hampshire.

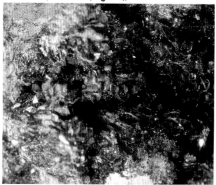

6 Natrojarosite, Greece, 8x

5 Beraunite

Hardness: 3–4.
Density: 2.9.
Streak: Yellow.
Chemical Formula:
$Fe_3[(OH)_3/(PO_4)_2] \cdot 2^{1}/_2\,H_2O$
Color: Yellow, green, brown, red; vitreous luster.
Cleavage: Good, but discernible only in relatively large crystals; fracture uneven.
Tenacity: Brittle.
Crystal Form: Monoclinic; tabular to acicular, radiating fibrous.
Occurrence: In phosphate pegmatites and limonite deposits.

Associated Minerals:
Cacoxenite, strengite, rockbridgeite, strunzite.
Similar Minerals: Yellow beraunite often cannot be distinguished from strunzite by ordinary methods.

6 Natrojarosite
Hardness: 3–4.
Density: 3.1–3.3.
Streak: Yellow.
Chemical Formula:
$NaFe_3(OH)_6/(SO_4)_2$
Color: Yellow to brown; vitreous luster.
Cleavage: Often discernibly basal; fracture uneven.
Tenacity: Brittle.

Crystal Form: Trigonal; tabular to rhombohedral, granular, powdery, crusty, as film, earthy, botryoidal.
Occurrence: In the oxidation zone.
Associated Minerals:
Goethite.
Similar Minerals:
Natrojarosite can be distinguished from jarosite only by chemical means. Beudantite is somewhat harder.

2 Pucherite, Schneeberg (Saxony, Germany), 8x

Minerals can be named for a great variety of things. Especially common are names that allude to a locality (pucherite, for the Pucher Shaft at Schneeberg) or to famous persons (nealite, for the American collector Neal Yedlin).

1 Walpurgite, Schneeberg (Saxony, Germany), 10x

1 Walpurgite

Hardness: 3¹/₂.
Density: 5.95.
Streak: Yellow.
Chemical Formula:
$(BiO)_4UO_2(AsO_4)_2 \cdot 3H_2O$
Color: Yellow to pale orange; greasy vitreous luster.
Cleavage: Perfect; fracture lamellar.
Tenacity: Brittle.
Crystal Form: Triclinic; tabular, radiating fibrous, earthy, crusty.
Occurrence: In uranium deposits.
Associated Minerals: Torbernite, zeunerite, bismutite.

Similar Minerals: Autunite and uranocircite have a different crystal form.

2 Pucherite

Hardness: 4.
Density: 6.25.
Streak: Yellow.
Chemical Formula: $Bi_2V_2O_8$
Color: Reddish brown to yellowish.
Cleavage: Perfect; fracture conchoidal.
Tenacity: Brittle.
Crystal Form: Orthorhombic; thick tabular, acicular, earthy, massive.
Occurrence: In the oxidation zone.

Associated Minerals: Bismuth, bismite.
Similar Minerals: Considering the paragenesis, there is no possibility of confusion with other minerals.

3 Nealite
Hardness: 4.
Density: 5.88.
Streak: Light orange-yellow.
Chemical Formula:
$Pb_4Fe(AsO_4)_2Cl_4$
Color: Yellow to orange-yellow; vitreous luster.
Cleavage: None; fracture uneven.
Tenacity: Brittle.
Crystal Form: Triclinic;

3 Nealite, Lavrion (Greece), 12x

4 Beudantite, Tsumeb (Namibia), 10x 5 Tsumcorite, Tsumeb (Namibia), 8x

prismatic, tabular, acicular.
Occurrence: In ancient lead slags.
Associated Minerals: Georgiadesite, paralaurionite.
Similar Minerals: Yellow paralaurionite has a different crystal form and is not brittle.

4 Beudantite
Hardness: 4.
Density: 4.3.
Streak: Yellow.
Chemical Formula: $PbFe_3[(OH)_6/SO_4/AsO_4]$
Color: Yellow, brown, greenish, olive; vitreous luster.
Cleavage: None; fracture conchoidal.

Tenacity: Brittle.
Crystal Form: Trigonal; rhombohedral, pseudocubic, tabular, crusty, earthy, massive.
Occurrence: In the oxidation zone.
Associated Minerals: Mimetite, jarosite, conichalcite.
Similar Minerals: Jarosite and natrojarosite are somewhat softer and have a cleavage.

5 Tsumcorite
Hardness: 4$^{1}/_{2}$.
Density: 5.2.
Streak: Yellowish.

Chemical Formula: $PbZnFe(AsO_4)_2 \cdot H_2O$
Color: Yellowish brown to orange; vitreous luster.
Cleavage: Not discernible; fracture uneven.
Tenacity: Brittle.
Crystal Form: Monoclinic; short prismatic, radiating fibrous, as crusts.
Occurrence: In the oxidation zone.
Associated Minerals: Malachite, cerussite, mimetite.
Similar Minerals: Mimetite has a different crystal form.

Brown

Minerals with a yellowish-brown to reddish-brown streak are described here.

If you are unsure whether the reddish-brown streak of a certain mineral places it in the brown or the red streak category, you will have to look in both groups.

Acicular rutile crystals, oriented and attached to hematite. Found at Ibitiara, Brazil. Specimen size, 2 inches (5 cm).

1 Berthierite, Romania, 0.2x

2 Baumhauerite, Switzerland, 8x

3 Descloizite, Berg Aukas (Namibia), 3x

1 Berthierite
Hardness: 2–3.
Density: 4.6.
Streak: Brownish gray.
Chemical Formula: $FeSb_2S_4$
Color: Steel-gray, often with yellow tarnish; metallic luster.
Cleavage: Discernible lengthwise; fracture uneven.
Tenacity: Brittle.
Crystal Form: Orthorhombic; acicular, fibrous, radiated.
Occurrence: In antimony ore veins.
Associated Minerals: Quartz, stibnite.
Similar Minerals: Stibnite is lighter in color and flexible but inelastic.

2 Baumhauerite
Hardness: 3.
Density: 5.33.
Streak: Brown.
Chemical Formula: $Pb_{12}As_{16}S_{36}$
Color: Steel-gray, often deep red internal reflections; metallic luster, occasionally dull.
Cleavage: Indistinct; fracture conchoidal.
Tenacity: Brittle.
Crystal Form: Triclinic; prismatic, usually with rounded edges.
Occurrence: In dolomite marble.
Associated Minerals: Dolomite, realgar, sartorite.
Similar Minerals: Sartorite has slanted pinacoid faces and no red internal reflections.

3 Descloizite
Hardness: 3¹/₂.
Density: 5.5–6.2.
Streak: Light brown.
Chemical Formula: $Pb(Zn,Cu)[OH/VO_4]$
Color: Brown, red, yellow, dark-brown; resinous luster.
Cleavage: None; fracture uneven.
Tenacity: Brittle.

Brown Streak

4 Sphalerite, Marburg (Germany), 5x

5 Sphalerite, Oelsnitz (Germany), 7x

Sphalerite is a mineral that can occur in an enormous range of colors. Different color variations have been given popular second names. For example, red sphalerite is also known as ruby blende.

6 Sphalerite, Rüdersdorf/Berlin (Germany), 2x

Crystal Form:
Orthorhombic; prismatic, more rarely tabular, often dendritic, radiating fibrous, crusty, massive.
Occurrence: In the oxidation zone.
Associated Minerals:
Vanadinite, wulfenite.
Similar Minerals: Magnetite is harder; brown calcite and smithsonite are lighter in weight and show a distinct cleavage.

4/5/6 Sphalerite
Hardness: 3¹/₂–4.
Density: 3.9–4.2.
Streak: Actually white, commonly yellow to brown if iron is present.
Chemical Formula: ZnS
Color: Yellow, brown, red, green, black, rarely colorless to white; semimetallic adamantine luster.
Cleavage: Perfect rhombic dodecahedral; fracture conchoidal.
Tenacity: Brittle.
Crystal Form: Isometric; often attached crystals, primarily tetrahedrons, rhombic dodecahedrons, often pseudo-octahedral, faces often striated, commonly twinned, radiating fibrous when massive, sparry, granular.
Occurrence: In granites, gabbros, contact metasomatic deposits, hydrothermal veins, and replacement deposits, in sedimentary and metamorphic deposits.
Associated Minerals:
Galena, pyrite, pyrrhotite.
Similar Minerals: Sphalerite differs from galena, garnet, tetrahedrite, and sulfur in hardness and cleavage.

1 Wurtzite, Oruro (Bolivia), 10x

2 Sartorite, Switzerland, 8x

3 Manganite, Harz Mountains
(Germany), 0.5x

1 Wurtzite

Hardness: 3¹/₂–4.
Density: 4.0.
Streak: Light brown.
Chemical Formula: ZnS
Color: Light brown to dark brown; resinous luster.
Cleavage: Basal and prismatic; fracture uneven.
Tenacity: Brittle.
Crystal Form: Hexagonal; capillary, pyramids with base, horizontally striated, radiated, compact.
Occurrence: In hydrothermal veins.
Accompanying Minerals: Sphalerite, galena, pyrite, marcasite.

Similar Minerals: Sphalerite has a different cleavage and crystal form.

2 Sartorite
Hardness: 3.
Density: 5.05.
Streak: Brown.
Chemical Formula: $PbAs_2S_4$
Color: Steel-gray; metallic luster.
Cleavage: Indistinct; fracture conchoidal.
Tenacity: Brittle.
Crystal Form: Monoclinic; prismatic with steep pinacoid face, often longitudinally grooved.
Occurrence: In druses in dolomite marble.
Associated Minerals: Dolomite, realgar, baumhauerite.
Similar Minerals: Baumhauerite usually has a larger number of rounded faces.

3 Manganite

Hardness: 4.
Density: 4.3–4.4.
Streak: Dark brown.
Chemical Formula: MnOOH
Color: Brownish black to black; metallic luster.
Cleavage: Distinct; fracture uneven.

4 Neptunite, California, 5x

5 Hausmannite, Ohrenstock (Thuringia, Germany), 8x

Hausmannite is a valuable manganese ore, from which manganese is obtained for use in steel refinement and other applications.

Tenacity: Brittle.
Crystal Form: Monoclinic; prismatic, tabular, radiating fibrous, earthy, massive.
Occurrence: In hydrothermal veins.
Associated Minerals: Pyrolusite, braunite, barite.
Similar Minerals: Goethite is a different color; pyrolusite has a pure-black streak.

4 Neptunite
Hardness: 5$^{1}/_{2}$.
Density: 3.23.
Streak: Brown.
Chemical Formula: $Na_2FeTi[Si_4O_{12}]$
Color: Black to dark brown; vitreous luster.
Cleavage: Usually not discernible; fracture splintery.
Tenacity: Brittle.
Crystal Form: Monoclinic; prismatic, massive.
Occurrence: In alkali pegmatites and natrolite veins.
Associated Minerals: Benitoite, aegerine, natrolite.
Similar Minerals: Tourmaline has a different crystal form and is harder.

5 Hausmannite
Hardness: 5$^{1}/_{2}$.
Density: 4.7–4.8.
Streak: Brown to reddish brown.
Chemical Formula: Mn_3O_4
Color: Iron-black, somewhat brownish; metallic luster.
Cleavage: Perfect; fracture uneven.
Tenacity: Brittle.
Crystal Form: Tetragonal; pseudo-octahedral, granular, massive.
Occurrence: In metamorphic manganese deposits, as lining in hydrothermal manganese ore veins.
Associated Minerals: Braunite, manganite.
Similar Minerals: Magnetite has a black streak; braunite has a much poorer cleavage.

2 Goethite, Ukraine, 1x

1 Goethite, Siegerland (Germany), 3x

3 Chromite, Turkey, 1x

1/2 Goethite
Hardness: 5–5^1/$_2$.
Density: 4.3.
Streak: Brown to brownish yellow.
Chemical Formula: FeOOH
Color: Yellow, brown to dark brown and reddish brown; metallic luster to dull.
Cleavage: Perfect, but often not discernible; fracture uneven.
Tenacity: Brittle.
Crystal Form: Orthorhombic; acicular, radiated, reniform with smooth surface (kidney ore), massive, earthy (limonite).
Occurrence: Crystals in vesicles in volcanic rocks, frequently in the oxidation zone.
Associated Minerals: Occurs in association with an extremely large number of minerals, particularly oxidation minerals.
Similar Minerals: Lepidocrocite is clearly more reddish and usually platy.

3 Chromite
Hardness: 5^1/$_2$.
Density: 4.5–4.8.
Streak: Brown.
Chemical Formula: $(Fe,Mg)Cr_2O_4$
Color: Brownish black to iron-black; metallic to greasy luster.
Cleavage: None; fracture conchoidal.
Tenacity: Brittle.
Crystal Form: Isometric; rarely octahedrons, usually granular, massive, embedded.
Occurrence: In basic rocks, in placers.
Associated Minerals: Olivine, magnetite, anorthite, pyroxene.
Similar Minerals: Magnetite has a black streak.

4 Wolframite, Zinnwald (Saxony, Germany), 1x

5 Huebnerite, Peru, 2x

The mineral goethite (opposite page) is named after the poet Johann Wolfgang von Goethe, whose many interests included geology and mineralogy. Portions of his mineral collection can be seen today in the German Museum in Munich.

6 Niccolite, Mansfeld (Germany), 4x

4/5 Wolframite

Hardness: 5–5¹/₂.
Density: 7.14–7.54.
Streak: Yellowish brown to dark brown, or black.
Chemical Formula: $(Fe,Mn)WO_4$. Forms a solid solution series with ferberite $(FeWO_4)$ and huebnerite $(MnWO_4)$ as the end members.
Color: Brown, reddish translucent (huebnerite) to black (ferberite); greasy, metallic luster.
Cleavage: Very good; fracture uneven.
Tenacity: Brittle.
Crystal Form: Monoclinic; tabular to prismatic, also acicular, sparry, massive.
Occurrence: In granites, pegmatites, pneumatolytic and hydrothermal veins.
Associated Minerals: Tourmaline, cassiterite, quartz, fluorite, apatite, arsenopyrite, molybdenite.
Similar Minerals: Columbite is somewhat harder and has a cleavage inferior to that of wolframite. Cassiterite has a different crystal form.

6 Niccolite

(Nickeline)

Hardness: 5¹/₂.
Density: 7.8.
Streak: Dark brown.
Chemical Formula: NiAs
Color: Metallic pink, with darker tarnish.
Cleavage: Usually not visible; fracture uneven.
Tenacity: Brittle to nonbrittle.
Crystal Form: Hexagonal; rarely pyramidal and fusiform crystals, almost always massive.
Occurrence: In hydrothermal ore veins and gabbros.
Associated Minerals: Maucherite, barite, arsenopyrite, annabergite.
Similar Minerals: Maucherite, much rarer, is somewhat lighter in color.

1 Aeschynite, Norway, 10x

2 Hypersthene, Adirondack Mountains, New York, 2x

Aeschynite contains elements from the group of rare earths. Depending on which element predominates, different minerals develop; their names are formed by adding the symbol of the dominant element to the end of the term—for example, aeschynite-(Ce) or aeschynite-(Y).

1 Aeschynite
Hardness: 5–6.
Density: 4.9–5.1.
Streak: Yellowish brown.
Chemical Formula:
$(Ce,Th,Ca)(Ti,Nb,Ta)_2O_6$
Color: Brown to iron-black (embedded), yellowish to brown translucent (attached); pitchy luster (embedded), vitreous luster (attached).
Cleavage: None, fracture conchoidal.
Tenacity: Brittle.
Crystal Form:
Orthorhombic; tabular to prismatic, massive, embedded.
Occurrence: In granite pegmatites.

Associated Minerals:
Xenotime, monazite, zircon.
Similar Minerals: Rutile has a tetragonal symmetry. Allanite (orthite) in attached crystals is more violet in color, and it has a different streak.

2 Hypersthene
Hardness: 5–6.
Density: 3.5.
Streak: Greenish white to brownish white.
Chemical Formula:
$(Fe,Mg)_2[Si_2O_6]$
Color: Black, dark brown, dark green; vitreous luster, often metallic gleam.

Cleavage: Discernible, often good parting; fracture uneven.
Tenacity: Brittle.
Crystal Form:
Orthorhombic; tabular to prismatic, lamellar, granular, massive.
Occurrence: In igneous rocks, metamorphic schists, pyroclasts.
Associated Minerals:
Olivine, diopside.
Similar Minerals: Bronzite and enstatite frequently cannot be distinguished from hypersthene by ordinary means.

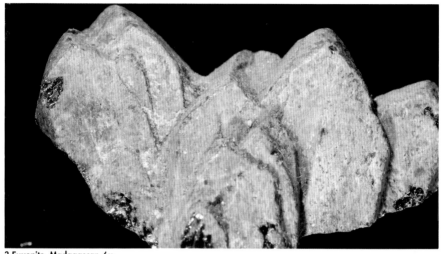

3 Euxenite, Madagascar, 6x

4 Hornblende, Zillertal (Austria), 1x

5 Hornblende, Eifel (Germany), 1x

3 Euxenite
Hardness: 5$\frac{1}{2}$–6$\frac{1}{2}$.
Density: 4.3–5.8.
Streak: Yellowish, brownish, gray.
Chemical Formula: $(Y,Ce,U)(Nb,Ta,Ti)_2O_6$
Color: Black, often with yellowish film; greasy luster.
Cleavage: None; fracture conchoidal.
Tenacity: Brittle.
Crystal Form: Orthorhombic; tabular, prismatic, massive.
Occurrence: In pegmatites.
Associated Minerals: Monazite, feldspar, quartz.
Similar Minerals: Monazite is not black.

4/5 Hornblende
Hardness: 5–6.
Density: 2.9–3.4.
Streak: Grayish green to grayish brown.
Chemical Formula: $(Ca,Na,K)_{2-3}(Mg,Fe,Al)_5$ $[(OH,F)_2/(Si,Al)_2Si_6O_{22}]$
Color: Dark green, black.
Cleavage: Perfect. Cleavage surfaces form an angle of about 120°. Fracture uneven.
Tenacity: Brittle.
Crystal Form: Monoclinic; prismatic, often with three-faced terminations, bladed, massive.
Occurrence: In granites, syenites, diorites, many volcanic rocks, fissures in volcanic rocks, and gneisses.
Associated Minerals: Biotite, augite, magnetite.
Similar Minerals: Augite has a different cleavage angle. Tourmaline has no cleavage.

81

1 Helvite, Schwarzenberg (Saxony, Germany), 10x

2 Franklinite, Franklin Hill, Sussex Co., New Jersey, 0.5x

Franklinite occurs chiefly in Franklin, New Jersey. This deposit is famous for its numerous fluorescent minerals, which occur with franklinite.

1 Helvite
Hardness: 6.
Density: 3.1–3.66.
Streak: Brownish.
Chemical Formula:
$(Fe,Mn,Zn)_8[S_2/(BeSiO_4)_6]$.
The terminal members of the solid solution series are danalite (Fe), helvite (Mn), and genthelvite (Zn).
Color: Light yellow, reddish brown, dark brownish red; vitreous luster.
Cleavage: None; fracture conchoidal.
Tenacity: Brittle.
Crystal Form: Isometric; tetrahedral, attached, embedded, granular, compact.

Occurrence: In skarn deposits.
Associated Minerals: Fluorite, garnet.
Similar Minerals: Tetrahedral crystals of helvite are quite characteristic. Garnet has a white streak. Sphalerite is softer and has distinct cleavage.

2 Franklinite
Hardness: 6.
Density: 5.0–5.2.
Streak: Reddish brown.
Chemical Formula:
$ZnFe_2O_4$
Color: Black; metallic luster.
Cleavage: None; fracture conchoidal.
Tenacity: Brittle.
Crystal Form: Isometric; usually octahedrons, massive, embedded.
Occurrence: In metamorphic zinc deposits.
Associated Minerals: Zincite, willemite, calcite.
Similar Minerals: Franklinite is distinguished from magnetite by its paragenesis with zinc minerals.

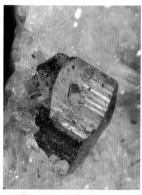

4 Babingtonite, India, 6x

3 Johannsenite, Broken Hill (Australia), 8x

Babingtonite is found in the quarries near Poona, India, in cavities in volcanic rocks, along with quartz, ilvaite, pumpellyite, and beautiful zeolite minerals.

3 Johannsenite
Hardness: 6.
Density: 3.4–3.6.
Streak: Brown.
Chemical Formula:
$Ca(Mn,Fe)Si_2O_6$
Color: Greenish, brown, black; vitreous luster.
Cleavage: Good; fracture conchoidal.
Tenacity: Brittle.
Crystal Form: Monoclinic; short prismatic, thick tabular, massive.
Occurrence: In metamorphic manganese deposits.
Associated Minerals: Rhodonite, bustamite.

Similar Minerals: Considering the paragenesis, confusion with other minerals is virtually impossible.

4 Babingtonite

Hardness: 5.
Density: 3.25–3.35.
Streak: Brownish black.
Chemical Formula:
$Ca_2FeFeSi_5O_{14}OH$
Color: Black; vitreous luster.
Cleavage: Perfect; fracture uneven.
Tenacity: Brittle.
Crystal Form: Triclinic; thick tabular to short prismatic.

Occurrence: Lining crevices in granite, in pegmatites and cavities in volcanic rocks.
Associated Minerals: Epidote, quartz, prehnite.
Similar Minerals: Axinite has a different streak and its color is usually lighter; moreover, its crystals tend to be brownish and translucent to transparent. Babingtonite, however, is typically black.

1 Ardennite, Saint-Chateau (Belgium), 10x

2 Pseudobrookite, USA, 6x

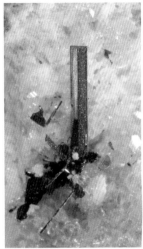

3 Braunite, Ilmenau (Germany), 6x

1 Ardennite

Hardness: 6.
Density: 3.62.
Streak: Yellowish brown.
Chemical Formula:
$Mn_5Al_5(As,V)O_4Si_5O_{20}$
$(OH)_2 \cdot 2H_2O$
Color: Yellowish brown; vitreous luster.
Cleavage: Perfect; fracture uneven.
Tenacity: Brittle.
Crystal Form:
Orthorhombic; radiated.
Occurrence: In metamorphic manganese deposits.
Associated Minerals:
Quartz, calcite.
Similar Minerals: Sursassite and saneroite are more reddish in color.

2 Pseudobrookite

Hardness: 6.
Density: 4.4.
Streak: Brownish to reddish, ocher-yellow.
Chemical Formula: Fe_2TiO_5
Color: Red, black, reddish black; metallic luster.
Cleavage: Scarcely discernible; fracture conchoidal.
Tenacity: Brittle.
Crystal Form:
Orthorhombic; prismatic to tabular, acicular.
Occurrence: In druses and cavities in volcanic rocks.
Associated Minerals:
Pyroxenite, hornblende, tridymite.
Similar Minerals:
Considering the paragenesis, any confusion is virtually impossible.

3 Braunite

Hardness: 6.
Density: 4.7–4.8.
Streak: Dark brown.
Chemical Formula:
$MnMn_6SiO_{12}$
Color: Black; metallic luster.
Cleavage: Perfect, but usually hard to discern; fracture uneven.
Tenacity: Brittle.

4 Rutile, Hohe Tauern (Austria), 6x

Rutile commonly forms twins. If twin formations appear repeatedly in an aggregate, stars, lattices, or even rings can result.

5 Rutile, Italy, 4x

Crystal Form: Tetragonal; pseudo-octahedral and pseudocubic, granular, massive.
Occurrence: In metamorphic manganese deposits.
Associated Minerals: Hausmannite, manganite.
Similar Minerals: Magnetite is distinctly magnetic. Hausmannite is often hard to distinguish by ordinary methods; typically, the crystal edges of this mineral are usually bent.

4/5 Rutile
Hardness: 6.
Density: 4.2–4.3.
Streak: Yellowish brown.
Chemical Formula: TiO_2
Color: Straw-yellow, yellowish brown, brownish red, red, black; luster adamantine to metallic.
Cleavage: Perfect prismatic, but visible only in thick crystals; fracture conchoidal.
Tenacity: Brittle.
Crystal Form: Tetragonal; prismatic to acicular, capillary, knee-shaped (geniculated) twins, reticulated shapes (sagenite).

Occurrence: In pegmatites; in sedimentary rocks, metamorphic rocks, and placers.
Associated Minerals: Anatase, brookite, titanite, hematite.
Similar Minerals: Tourmaline is harder and has a different luster. Magnetite has a different streak. Brookite and anatase have a different crystal form.

Green

Minerals with a light green, bluish green, grayish green to blackish green streak are found on the pages that follow.

Many of these minerals, which also have a green body color, are compounds of copper, which is responsible for the green color. For this reason, an especially large number of minerals that are created during the weathering of copper ores are included in the following group.

Globular malachite from Neuer Muth Mine at Nanzenbach, near Dillenburg (Germany). Width, about $2^1/_2$ inches (6 cm).

1 Tyrolite, Brixlegg (Tyrol, Austria), 6x

2 Chalcophyllite, Chile, 6x

The mineral tyrolite was named for the Tyrol, where it was first found, in relatively large quantities, in the mining regions of Schwaz and Brixlegg.

3 Ktenasite, Iserlohn (Germany), 12x

1 Tyrolite
Hardness: 2.
Density: 3.2.
Streak: Bluish green.
Chemical Formula:
$Ca_2Cu_9[(OH)_{10}/(AsO_4)_4] \cdot 10H_2O$
Color: Bluish green to light green; pearly luster.
Cleavage: Perfect; fracture lamellar.
Tenacity: Nonbrittle, plates flexible.
Crystal Form: Orthorhombic; thin tabular, often intergrown to form rosettes, massive, crusty, as coat.
Occurrence: In the oxidation zone.
Associated Minerals: Brochantite, langite, posnjakite.
Similar Minerals: Brochantite is pure green in color; azurite is darker blue; chalcophyllite has a different crystal form.

2 Chalcophyllite
Hardness: 2.
Density: 2.67.
Streak: Greenish.
Chemical Formula:
$Cu_{18}Al_2[(OH)_{27}/(AsO_4)_3/(SO_4)_3] \cdot 36H_2O$
Color: Bluish green to emerald green; vitreous luster.
Cleavage: Perfect; fracture lamellar.
Tenacity: Flexible.
Crystal Form: Hexagonal; thin tabular, six-sided lamellae, also as rosettes, crusts.
Occurrence: In the oxidation zone.
Associated Minerals: Devillite, malachite, spangolite, tyrolite.
Similar Minerals: Minerals with a green streak do not form thin six-sided plates.

3 Ktenasite
Hardness: $2-2^1/_2$.
Density: 2.9.
Streak: Greenish.

4 Chlorite, Ankogel (Germany), 5x

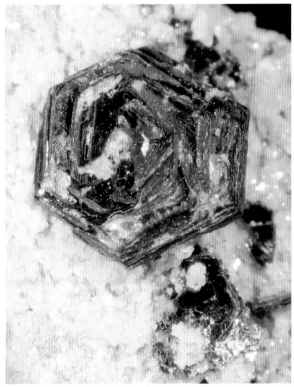

5 Chlorite, Val Casaccia (Switzerland), 5x

Chlorite is characteristically dark green to olive green. Often a band of chlorite in the rock indicates that a cavity with beautifully crystallized minerals is located deep within.

Chemical Formula:
$(Cu,Zn)_3(SO_4)(OH)_4 \cdot 2H_2O$
Color: Bluish green, green; vitreous luster.
Cleavage: Discernible; fracture uneven.
Tenacity: Brittle.
Crystal Form: Monoclinic; tabular, crusty.
Occurrence: In the oxidation zone.
Associated Minerals: Glaucokerinite, serpierite.
Similar Minerals: Glaucokerinite is softer and acicular.

4/5 Chlorite

Hardness: 2.
Density: 2.6–3.3 (depending on iron content).
Streak: Green, more rarely brown.
Chemical Formula:
$(Fe,Mg,Al)_6[(OH)_2/(Si,Al)_4O_{10}]$.
The chlorites form a solid solution series with four theoretical end members; the formula above is highly generalized.
Color: Dark green to brown; vitreous luster, on cleavage surfaces luster is pearly.
Cleavage: Perfect basal; fracture lamellar.
Tenacity: Nonbrittle, flexible but inelastic.
Crystal Form: Monoclinic; thin to thick tabular, vermiform, granular, arenaceous.
Occurrence: Rock-forming in metamorphic rocks (chlorite schists) and sediments.
Associated Minerals: Grossular, rutile, mica, vesuvianite, diopside.
Similar Minerals: Micas are harder, and they are flexible and elastic.

1 Torbernite, Cornwall (England), 6x

2 Zeunerite, Black Forest (Germany), 8x

Torbernite and zeunerite belong to the uranium mica group. The name of the group is attributable to these minerals' uranium content and to the fact that they all display a micaceous cleavage.

1 Torbernite
Hardness: 2–2¹/₂.
Density: 3.3–3.7.
Streak: Green.
Chemical Formula:
$Cu[UO_2/PO_4]_2 \cdot 8–12H_2O$
Color: Emerald green; vitreous luster, pearly luster on cleavage surfaces.
Cleavage: Perfect; fracture uneven.
Tenacity: Brittle to nonbrittle.
Crystal Form: Tetragonal; thin to thick tabular, bipyramidal, attached, earthy, crusty.
Occurrence: In the oxidation zone, as coating of fissures in granites.

Associated Minerals:
Autunite, uranocircite, fluorite, barite.
Similar Minerals: Autunite and uranocircite fluoresce, unlike torbernite, and they tend to be yellower. Zeunerite is indistinguishable by ordinary methods, but the paragenesis with arsenic-containing minerals is indicative.

2 Zeunerite
Hardness: 2–2¹/₂.
Density: 3.79.
Streak: Green.
Chemical Formula:
$Cu[UO_2/AsO_4]_2 \cdot 8–12H_2O$
Color: Emerald green; vitreous luster, on cleavage surfaces pearly luster.
Cleavage: Perfect basal; fracture uneven.
Tenacity: Brittle to nonbrittle.
Crystal Form: Tetragonal; tabular to bipyramidal, crusty, earthy.
Occurrence: In the oxidation zone.
Associated Minerals:
Heinrichite, barite, fluorite.
Similar Minerals: Zeunerite is indistinguishable from torbernite by ordinary methods, but the paragenesis with other arsenic-containing minerals usually is indicative.

3 Devillite, Harz Mountains (Germany), 10x

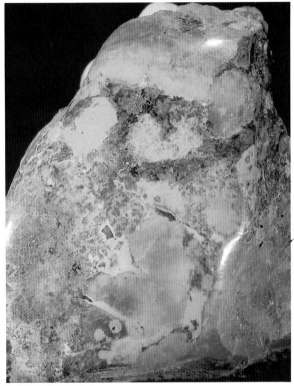

Chrysocolla is often cut and polished for use as jewelry because of its intense color and the frequently interesting marking. Chrysocolla from Israel is often called Eilat stone, after the town of Eilat, near the site of occurrence.

4 Chrysocolla, Israel, 2x

3 Devillite
Hardness: $2^1/_2$.
Density: 3.13.
Streak: Pale green.
Chemical Formula: $CaCu_4[(OH)_6/(SO_4)_2] \cdot 3H_2O$
Color: Emerald green to bluish green, light blue to whitish; luster vitreous to pearly.
Cleavage: Perfect; fracture lamellar.
Tenacity: Flexible.
Crystal Form: Monoclinic; six-sided striated lamellae, globular, crusty, foamy.
Occurrence: In the oxidation zone.

Associated Minerals: Tyrolite, posnjakite, langite.
Similar Minerals: Chalcophyllite is bluer. Serpierite frequently is indistinguishable by ordinary methods.

4 Chrysocolla
Hardness: 2–4.
Density: 2.0–2.2.
Streak: Greenish white.
Chemical Formula: $CuSiO_3$
Color: Light blue, blue, greenish blue; vitreous luster, slightly greasy.
Cleavage: None; fracture conchoidal.
Tenacity: Brittle.

Crystal Form: Usually amorphous; botryoidal, reniform masses, massive.
Occurrence: In the oxidation zone.
Associated Minerals: Cuprite, malachite, azurite, limonite.
Similar Minerals: Malachite is a different color.

Green Streak

1 Olivenite, Wheal Gorland Mine (Cornwall, England), 6x

2 Clinoclase, Cornwall (England), 5x

Wheal Gorland Mine in Cornwall, now long in disuse, is famous worldwide for having provided a great many excellent oxidation minerals.

1 Olivenite
(Leucochalcite)
Hardness: 3.
Density: 4.3.
Streak: Yellowish green to olive green.
Chemical Formula: $Cu_2[OH/AsO_4]$
Color: Light green to olive green, blackish green, brown, whitish; luster vitreous to silky.
Cleavage: None; fracture conchoidal.
Tenacity: Brittle.
Crystal Form: Orthorhombic; tabular to prismatic, acicular, capillary, fibrous, radiated, botryoidal, reniform, earthy.
Occurrence: In the oxidation zone.
Associated Minerals: Cornwallite, clinoclase, azurite, malachite.
Similar Minerals: Adamite is usually much lighter green, but its copper-containing variety, copper adamite, is often quite difficult to distinguish. The same is true of libethenite; here, however, the paragenesis with other phosphorous-containing minerals is indicative.

2 Clinoclase
Hardness: 2¹/₂–3.
Density: 4.2–4.4.
Streak: Bluish green.
Chemical Formula: $Cu_3[(OH)_3/AsO_4]$
Color: Greenish blue to dark faded blue; vitreous luster.
Cleavage: Perfect basal; fracture lamellar.
Tenacity: Brittle.
Crystal Form: Monoclinic; prismatic to tabular, radiated, reniform, crusty, as coat.
Occurrence: In the oxidation zone.
Associated Minerals: Olivenite, azurite, malachite.
Similar Minerals: Azurite is

3 Libethenite, Cornwall (England), 3x

Tsumeb in Namibia is one of the most famous mineral sites, where numerous mineral species have been found. Some of the best specimens of other mineral species—azurite, for example—ever discovered anywhere have come from Tsumeb.

4 Mottramite, Tsumeb (Namibia), 8x

a purer blue and has a blue streak.

3 Libethenite

Hardness: 4.
Density: 3.8.
Streak: Olive green.
Chemical Formula:
$Cu_2[OH/PO_4]$
Color: Dark green to blackish green; vitreous luster.
Cleavage: None; fracture conchoidal.
Tenacity: Brittle.
Crystal Form:
Orthorhombic; prismatic to frequently pseudo-octahedral, attached, radiating fibrous, reniform, crusty.

Occurrence: In the oxidation zone.
Associated Minerals:
Euchroite, pseudomalachite.
Similar Minerals:
Cuproadamite and olivenite are virtually indistinguishable from libethenite by ordinary methods, but their paragenesis with arsenic-containing minerals is clearly indicative.

4 Mottramite

Hardness: $3^1/_2$.
Density: 5.7–6.2.
Streak: Green.
Chemical Formula:
$Pb(Cu,Zn)[OH/VO_4]$
Color: Olive green to dark green; resinous luster.
Cleavage: None; fracture uneven.
Tenacity: Brittle.
Crystal Form:
Orthorhombic; rarely prismatic, usually radiated, crusty, dendritic.
Occurrence: In the oxidation zone.
Associated Minerals:
Descloizite, azurite, malachite.
Similar Minerals:
Descloizite is more brown. Malachite effervesces with hydrochloric acid and is more emerald green.

1 Atacamite, La Farola (Chile), 10x

2 Mixite, France, 8x

Atacamite, a copper chloride, is common primarily in the oxidation zone of copper deposits in desert regions. It was named for one of the most desolate of these regions, the Atacama Desert in Chile.

1 Atacamite
Hardness: 3–3½.
Density: 3.76.
Streak: Green.
Chemical Formula: $Cu_2(OH)_3Cl$
Color: Emerald green to blackish green; vitreous luster.
Cleavage: Perfect; fracture conchoidal.
Tenacity: Brittle.
Crystal Form: Orthorhombic; prismatic, acicular, rarely tabular, radiated, lamellar, crusty, massive as an efflorescence.
Occurrence: In the oxidation zone.

Associated Minerals: Cuprite, malachite, native copper.
Similar Minerals: Malachite effloresces with hydrochloric acid; brochantite is somewhat harder and not so dark green.

2 Mixite
Hardness: 3–4.
Density: 3.8.
Streak: Green.
Chemical Formula: $(Bi,CaH)Cu_6[(OH)_6/(AsO_4)_3] \cdot 3H_2O$
Color: Bluish green to yellowish green; luster vitreous to silky.
Cleavage: Not discernible; fracture fibrous.
Tenacity: Brittle.
Crystal Form: Hexagonal; acicular, capillary, radiating fibrous, earthy, massive.
Occurrence: In the oxidation zone.
Associated Minerals: Pharmacosiderite, zeunerite, emplectite.
Similar Minerals: Agardite is not easy to distinguish by ordinary methods, but the paragenesis with bismuth ores often provides pointers.

Green Streak

3–4

3 Agardite-(La), Lavrion (Greece), 10x

4 Agardite-(Ce), Clara Mine, Black Forest (Germany), 6x

5 Euchroite, Libethen (Czechoslovakia), 8x

3/4 Agardite
Hardness: 3–4.
Density: 3.6–3.7.
Streak: Greenish.
Chemical Formula:
$(RE,Ca)_2Cu_{12}[(OH)_{12}/(AsO_4)_6] \cdot 6H_2O$.
The minerals of the agardite group are named according to the dominant element in the group of rare earths (RE). The mineral with lanthanum predominant is called agardite-(La); with cerium predominant it is known as agardite-(Ce). In general, the minerals of this group are also commonly known as chlorotile.

Color: Yellowish green to bluish green.
Cleavage: Not discernible; fracture uneven, fibrous.
Tenacity: Brittle.
Crystal Form: Hexagonal; acicular tufts.
Occurrence: Oxidation zone.
Associated Minerals: Adamite, olivenite, limonite.
Similar Minerals: Differentiating among the individual agardite minerals and distinguishing them from mixite is impossible by ordinary methods; otherwise, they are quite characteristic. Malachite effervesces with hydrochloric acid.

5 Euchroite
Hardness: $3^1/_2$–4.
Density: 3.45.
Streak: Green.
Chemical Formula:
$Cu_2AsO_4OH \cdot 3H_2O$
Color: Green; vitreous luster.
Cleavage: Not discernible; fracture conchoidal.
Tenacity: Brittle.
Crystal Form: Orthorhombic; prismatic to tabular.
Occurrence: In the oxidation zone.
Associated Minerals: Libethenite, azurite, malachite.
Similar Minerals: Libethenite has a different crystal form.

95

Green Streak

1 Arsentsumebite, Tsumeb (Namibia), 10x

2 Spangolite, Lavrion (Greece), 8x

Frequently there are minerals that differ from each other by only one element: Such a pair are the extremely rare phosphate tsumebite and the more common arsenate arsentsumebite.

3 Arthurite, Cornwall (England), 12x

1 Arsentsumebite
Hardness: 3.
Density: 6.0–6.1.
Streak: Green.
Chemical Formula:
$Pb_2Cu(AsO_4)(SO_4)OH$
Color: Green; vitreous luster.
Cleavage: None; fracture uneven.
Tenacity: Brittle.
Crystal Form: Monoclinic; tabular, as crusts.
Occurrence: In the oxidation zone.
Associated Minerals: Azurite, cerussite.
Similar Minerals: Devillite and chalcophyllite are not brittle.

2 Spangolite
Hardness: 3.
Density: 3.14.
Streak: Pale green.
Chemical Formula:
$Cu_6AlSO_4(OH)_{12}Cl \cdot 3H_2O$
Color: Dark green to bluish green, vitreous luster.
Cleavage: Perfect; fracture uneven.
Tenacity: Brittle.
Crystal Form: Hexagonal; thick tabular, as crusts.
Tenacity: Brittle.
Occurrence: In the oxidation zone.
Associated Minerals: Serpierite, brochantite, azurite.

Similar Minerals: Chalcophyllite has thin tabular crystals.

3 Arthurite
Hardness: 3–4.
Density: 3.02.
Streak: Greenish.
Chemical Formula:
$Cu_2Fe_4(AsO_4)_4(O,OH)_4 \cdot 8H_2O$
Color: Green; vitreous luster.
Cleavage: Not discernible; fracture uneven.
Tenacity: Brittle.
Crystal Form: Monoclinic; prismatic, acicular.
Occurrence: In the oxidation zone.

4 Brochantite, Chile, 6x

Brochantite is distinguished from the very similar mineral malachite by the hydrochloric acid test: Unlike malachite, brochantite does not effervesce with cold diluted HCl.

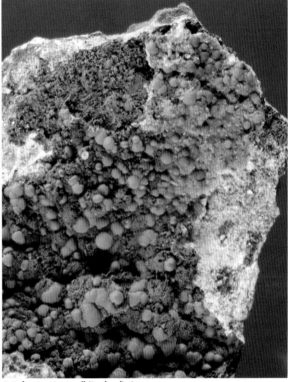

5 Dufrenite, Cornwall (England), 8x

Associated Minerals:
Pharmacosiderite, beudantite.
Similar Minerals: Olivenite is similar.

4 Brochantite
Hardness: $3^1/_2$–4.
Density: 3.97.
Streak: Green to light green.
Chemical Formula:
$Cu_4[(OH)_6/SO_4]$
Color: Emerald green; vitreous luster, on cleavage surfaces luster is pearly.
Cleavage: Perfect, but usually not discernible because of the acicular crystals; fracture uneven.
Tenacity: Brittle.

Crystal Form: Monoclinic; acicular, more rarely tabular, radiating fibrous, reniform, granular, earthy.
Occurrence: Oxidation zone.
Associated Minerals: Malachite, azurite, langite, posnjakite.
Similar Minerals: Malachite effervesces with hydrochloric acid. Atacamite is softer and usually somewhat darker.

5 Dufrenite
Hardness: $3^1/_2$–4.
Density: 3.1–3.3.
Streak: Green.
Chemical Formula:
$Fe^{+2}Fe_4^{+3}(OH)_5(PO_4)_3 \cdot H_2O$

Color: Yellowish green to dark green, turns brown with oxidation; luster vitreous to dull.
Cleavage: Perfect; fracture uneven.
Tenacity: Brittle.
Crystal Form: Monoclinic; thick tabular, as radiated crusts, globular.
Occurrence: In phosphate pegmatites.
Associated Minerals: Hureaulite, laubmannite, rockbridgeite.
Similar Minerals: Rockbridgeite is blacker, but often indistinguishable from dufrenite by ordinary methods.

2 Malachite, Harz (Germany), 4x

1 Malachite, Friedrich Mine (Siegerland, Germany), 4x

3 Rosasite, Arizona, 6x

1/2 Malachite

Hardness: 4.
Density: 4.0.
Streak: Green.
Chemical Formula:
$Cu_2[(OH)_2/CO_3]$
Color: Emerald green to light green. Vitreous luster, silky in aggregates, also dull.
Cleavage: Good, but rarely seen because of the usually acicular or fibrous develop-ment of the crystals; fracture conchoidal.
Tenacity: Brittle.
Crystal Form: Monoclinic; acicular bunches, tabular, fibrous, radiated, as reniform crusts, massive, earthy.

Occurrence: In the oxidation zone.
Associated Minerals: Limonite, azurite.
Special Property: Effervesces with dilute hydrochloric acid.
Similar Minerals: Minerals that might be confused with malachite are not soluble in dilute hydrochloric acid with effervescence.

3 Rosasite

Hardness: 4.
Density: 4.0
Streak: Bluish green.
Chemical Formula:
$(Cu,Zn)_2[(OH)_2/CO_3]$

Color: Green with blue cast; vitreous luster.
Cleavage: Not discernible because of the acicular or fibrous development of the crystals; fracture fibrous.
Tenacity: Brittle.
Crystal Form: Monoclinic; always acicular, radiating fibrous, as crusts.
Occurrence: In the oxidation zone.
Associated Minerals: Hemimorphite, aurichalcite, smithsonite.
Special Property: Effervesces with dilute hydrochloric acid.
Similar Minerals: Malachite

4 Pseudomalachite, Bavaria, 6x

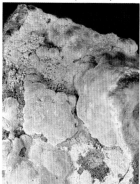

5 Kidwellite, Arkansas, 4x

6 Pseudomalachite, Nizhniy Tagil'sk (Russia), 2x

is bluish green without a blue cast. Chrysocolla does not effervesce with dilute hydrochloric acid.

4/6 Pseudomalachite
Hardness: $4^1/_2$.
Density: 4.34.
Streak: Green.
Chemical Formula:
$Cu_5[(OH)_2/PO_4]_2$
Color: Dark green to blackish green; vitreous to greasy luster.
Cleavage: None; fracture conchoidal.
Tenacity: Brittle.
Crystal Form: Monoclinic; tabular, often radiating fibrous, reniform, crusty, earthy.
Occurrence: In the oxidation zone.
Associated Minerals: Malachite, libethenite.
Similar Minerals: Malachite effervesces when moistened with dilute hydrochloric acid. Cornwallite is indistinguishable by ordinary methods, but the paragenesis with arsenic-containing minerals is always indicative.

5 Kidwellite
Hardness: 4.
Density: 2.5.
Streak: Greenish.
Chemical Formula:
$NaFe_9(PO_4)_6(OH)_{10} \cdot 5H_2O$
Color: Yellowish green; vitreous luster.
Cleavage: Not discernible; fracture fibrous.
Tenacity: Brittle.
Crystal Form: Monoclinic; fibrous, radiating fibrous crusts.
Occurrence: In phosphate deposits.
Associated Minerals: Rockbridgeite, strengite.
Similar Minerals: Beraunite usually forms only a few tufts and no compact crusts.

1 Conichalcite, Lavrion (Greece), 6x

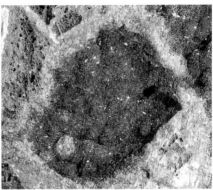

3 Chalcosiderite, Cornwall (England), 4x

2 Bayldonite, Cornwall (England), 6x

Many copper oxidation minerals are green in color because of their copper content.

1 Conichalcite

Hardness: 4¹/₂.
Density: 4.33.
Streak: Light green.
Chemical Formula:
$CaCu[OH/AsO_4]$
Color: Light green to apple green; vitreous luster.
Cleavage: Not discernible; fracture uneven.
Tenacity: Brittle.
Crystal Form:
Orthorhombic; acicular, radiating fibrous, reniform, warty, crusty.
Occurrence: In the oxidation zone.
Associated Minerals:
Copper adamite, olivenite, beudantite.
Similar Minerals: The apple-green color is quite characteristic.

2 Bayldonite

Hardness: 4¹/₂.
Density: 5.5.
Streak: Green.
Chemical Formula:
$PbCu_3[OH/AsO_4]_2$
Color: Green to yellowish green; resinous luster.
Cleavage: None; fracture uneven.
Tenacity: Brittle.
Crystal Form: Monoclinic; thick tabular, crusty, radiating fibrous.

Occurrence: In the oxidation zone of ore veins.
Associated Minerals:
Mimetite, azurite, duftite.
Similar Minerals: Malachite is always acicular. Olivenite has a different crystal form.

3 Chalcosiderite

Hardness: 4¹/₂.
Density: 3.22.
Streak: Green.
Chemical Formula:
$CuFe_6[(OH)_8/(PO_4)_4] \cdot 4H_2O$
Color: Dark green; vitreous luster.
Cleavage: Perfect; fracture uneven.
Tenacity: Brittle.

4 Cornwallite, Cornwall (England), 8x

Rockbridgeite often forms black to greenish black masses with a smooth surface and a green streak.

5 Rockbridgeite, Siegerland (Germany), 6x

Crystal Form: Triclinic; short prismatic to thick tabular, as crusts, massive.
Occurrence: Oxidation zone.
Associated Minerals: Malachite, olivenite, libethenite.
Similar Minerals: Olivenite and libethenite have a different crystal form.

4 Cornwallite
Hardness: 4½–5.
Density: 4–4.1.
Streak: Green.
Chemical Formula: $Cu_5[(OH)_2/AsO_4]_2$
Color: Green; vitreous luster.
Cleavage: None; fracture conchoidal.

Tenacity: Brittle.
Crystal Form: Monoclinic; tabular, radiating fibrous.
Occurrence: Oxidation zone.
Associated Minerals: Olivenite, chlorotile, clinoclase.
Similar Minerals: Malachite effervesces with dilute hydrochloric acid. Pseudomalachite is indistinguishable by ordinary methods.

5 Rockbridgeite
Hardness: 4½.
Density: 3.4.
Streak: Green to brown.
Chemical Formula: $(Fe,Mn)Fe_4[(OH)_5/(PO_4)_3]$

Color: Black, blackish green, brown; vitreous luster.
Cleavage: Poor; fracture uneven.
Tenacity: Brittle.
Crystal Form: Orthorhombic; prismatic, tabular, often radiating fibrous, resembling limonite, reniform, crusty, massive.
Occurrence: In phosphate pegmatites and limonite deposits.
Associated Minerals: Beraunite, strengite.
Similar Minerals: The color and streak are quite characteristic.

2 Actinolite, Habachtal (Austria), 3x

3 Actinolite, Zillertal (Austria), 0.5x

1 Dioptase, Altyn Tyube (Kazakhstan), 2x

1 Dioptase

Hardness: 5.
Density: 3.3.
Streak: Green.
Chemical Formula:
$Cu_6[Si_6O_{18}] \cdot 6H_2O$
Color: Emerald green;
vitreous luster.
Cleavage: Discernible
rhombohedral; fracture
conchoidal.
Tenacity: Brittle.
Crystal Form: Trigonal;
prismatic.
Occurrence: In the oxidation
zone.
Associated Minerals:
Malachite, azurite, duftite,
wulfenite, cerussite.

Similar Minerals: Malachite
has a different crystal form
and effervesces with dilute
hydrochloric acid.

2/3 Actinolite
Hardness: $5^1/_2$–6.
Density: 2.9–3.1.
Streak: Greenish.
Chemical Formula:
$(Ca,Fe)_2(Mg,Fe)_5[OH/Si4O_{11}]_2$
Color: Light green to dark
green; vitreous luster.
Cleavage: Perfect, cleavage
angle about 120°; fracture
uneven.
Tenacity: Brittle.
Crystal Form: Monoclinic;
bladed to acicular, radiated

(actinolite) to fibrous, capillary (amianthus, byssolite).
Occurrence: In talc and
chlorite schists, eclogites.
Associated Minerals: Talc,
mica, calcite, epidote.
Similar Minerals: Pyroxenes
have a different cleavage
angle. Tourmaline has a
different crystal form and no
cleavage.

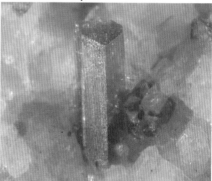

5 Gadolinite, Norway, 2x

4 Augite, Eifel (Germany), 2x

Gadolinite is a much-sought-after rare mineral of Alpine cavities, where it occurs in green, translucent to transparent crystals. In pegmatites, however, gadolinite is always black and opaque.

6 Gadolinite, Gasteiner Tal (Austria), 10x

4 Augite
Hardness: 6.
Density: 3.3–3.5.
Streak: Greenish.
Chemical Formula:
$(Ca,Mg,Fe)_2[(Si,Al)_2O_6]$
Color: Dark green, black; vitreous luster.
Cleavage: Distinctly prismatic; cleavage angle approximately 90°; fracture conchoidal.
Tenacity: Brittle.
Crystal Form: Monoclinic; short to long prismatic, acicular, granular, massive.
Occurrence: In volcanic rocks.

Associated Minerals: Biotite, olivine, hornblende.
Similar Minerals: Hornblende has a different cleavage and is more hexagonal in cross section.

5/6 Gadolinite
Hardness: 6¹/₂.
Density: 4.0–4.7.
Streak: Greenish.
Chemical Formula:
$Y_2FeBe_2[O/SiO_4]$
Color: Black, opaque; green, transparent. Pitchy to vitreous luster.
Cleavage: Usually not discernible; fracture conchoidal.

Tenacity: Brittle.
Crystal Form: Monoclinic; massive, embedded (opaque; pitchy luster), prismatic, attached (transparent; vitreous luster).
Occurrence: In pegmatites.
Associated Minerals: Synchysite, aeschynite, xenotime, monazite.
Similar Minerals: Green, embedded gadolinite is unmistakable; black, embedded gadolinite can be distinguished from other black minerals by its streak.

Black

Minerals whose streak is gray to black are discussed on the following pages.

In isolated cases, to make a definite identification it may be necessary to rub the streak with the corner of a second streak plate, in order to see the differences in shade more clearly. Where this is essential for accurate identification of a mineral, it is noted in the profile.

This group includes many important ore minerals, such as chalcopyrite, galena, chalcocite, and stibnite.

Chalcopyrite crystals up to about 3/4 inch (2 cm), from the Stahlberg Mine near Musen in the Siegerland (Germany).

105

2 Graphite, Sweden, 8x

Nagyagite is a rare gold mineral, named for former Nagyag (now Sacaramb) Romania, where it was found.

1 Nagyagite, Sacaramb (Romania), 6x

1 Nagyagite
Hardness: 1–1¹/₂.
Density: 7.4–7.6.
Streak: Dark gray.
Chemical Formula:
$Au(Pb,Sb,Fe)_8(Te,S)_{11}$
Color: Dark lead-gray; metallic luster.
Cleavage: Perfect basal; fracture hackly.
Tenacity: Flexible in thin sheets.
Crystal Form: Orthorhombic, pseudotetragonal; tabular, lamellar.
Occurrence: In subvolcanic gold ore veins.
Associated Minerals: Krennerite, sylvanite, native gold.
Similar Minerals: Molybdenite has a different streak; graphite leaves a mark on paper.

2 Graphite
Hardness: 1.
Density: 2.1–2.3.
Streak: Gray, metallic.
Chemical Formula: C
Color: Dark to light steel-gray, opaque; luster metallic to dull.
Cleavage: Perfect basal; fracture lamellar.
Tenacity: Flexible, nonbrittle.
Crystal Form: Hexagonal; tabular, usually only embedded lamellae, compact, earthy, scaly.
Occurrence: In crystalline schists, marbles, pegmatites.
Associated Minerals: Calcite, wollastonite.
Special Property: Leaves mark on paper.
Similar Minerals: Molybdenite is harder.

3/5 Molybdenite
Hardness: 1–1¹/₂.
Density: 4.7–4.8.
Streak: Dark gray.
Chemical Formula: MoS_2
Color: Lead-gray, opaque; metallic luster.
Cleavage: Perfect; fracture

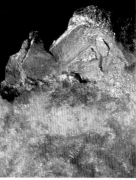

3 Molybdenite, Zillertal (Austria), 2x

5 Molybdenite, Lusatia (Germany), 4x

4 Covellite, Sardinia (Italy), 2x

lamellar.
Tenacity: Flexible but inelastic, nonbrittle.
Crystal Form: Hexagonal; rarely tabular crystals, usually embedded lamellae, scaly, massive.
Occurrence: In pegmatites, pneumatolytic formations, quartz veins, granite rocks.
Associated Minerals: Quartz, pyrite, wolframite.
Similar Minerals: The rubbed streak of graphite is more metallic and rather brownish. Hematite has a red streak, ilmenite a brown one, and these minerals are much harder and brittle.

4 Covellite
Hardness: $1\frac{1}{2}$–2.
Density: 4.68.
Streak: Blue-black.
Chemical Formula: CuS
Color: Blue-black, opaque; metallic luster.
Cleavage: Perfect basal; fracture lamellar.
Tenacity: Nonbrittle; thin sheets are flexible.
Crystal Form: Hexagonal; tabular to lamellar, usually massive, crusty, earthy, as coatings.
Occurrence: In hydrothermal veins, as coating on other sulfides.
Associated Minerals: Pyrite,

chalcopyrite, chalcocite.
Special Property: Color turns to violet when moistened with water.
Similar Minerals: The blue-black color and the change of color when wet are characteristic.

1 Sylvanite, Sacaramb (Romania), 8x

2 Polybasite, Freiburg (Ger.), 3x

3 Emplectite, Pforzheim (Ger.), 6x

1 Sylvanite
Hardness: 1½–2.
Density: 8.0–8.3.
Streak: Gray.
Chemical Formula:
$AgAuTe_4$
Color: Silvery gray, whitish, often with darker tarnish; metallic luster.
Cleavage: Perfect; fracture uneven.
Tenacity: Nonbrittle.
Crystal Form: Monoclinic; prismatic to tabular, often striated, rarely massive.
Occurrence: In hydrothermal veins.
Associated Minerals: Nagyagite, krennerite,

calaverite.
Similar Minerals:
Tetradymite has a different crystal form.

2 Polybasite
Hardness: 1½–2.
Density: 6.0–6.2.
Streak: Black to slightly reddish.
Chemical Formula:
$(Ag,Cu)_{16}Sb_2S_{11}$
Color: Iron-black, reddish translucent on the edges; metallic luster.
Cleavage: Perfect basal; fracture uneven.
Tenacity: Nonbrittle.
Crystal Form: Monoclinic,

pseudohexagonal; six-sided plates with triangular striation, massive.
Occurrence: In silver ore veins.
Associated Minerals:
Argentite, native silver, pyrargyrite, stephanite.
Similar Minerals:
Stephanite is somewhat harder, lacks triangular striation, and has poor cleavage.

3 Emplectite
Hardness: 2.
Density: 6.38.
Streak: Black.
Chemical Formula: $CuBiS_2$
Color: Steel-gray, tarnishing

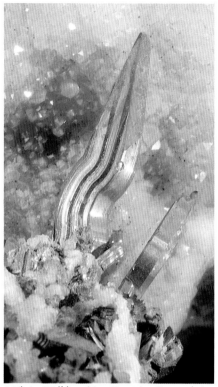

5 Stibnite, Wolfsberg (Harz Mountains, Germany), 3x

4 Stibnite, Wolfsberg (Harz Mountains, Germany), 4x   6 Stibnite, Siegerland (Germany), 1x

to yellow; metallic luster.
Cleavage: Frequently visible; fracture uneven.
Tenacity: Nonbrittle.
Crystal Form:
Orthorhombic; acicular to radiated, massive, embedded.
Ocurrence: In hydrothermal veins, particularly those of bismuth-cobalt-nickel formation.
Associated Minerals:
Wittichenite, skutterudite, barite, quartz.
Similar Minerals:
Emplectite usually cannot be distinguished from other sulfosalts by ordinary methods. Wittichenite is somewhat

blacker and has no cleavage.

4/5/6 Stibnite
(Antimonite)
Hardness: 2.
Density: 4.6–4.7.
Streak: Dark gray.
Chemical Formula: Sb_2S_3
Color: Lead-gray, opaque; metallic luster.
Cleavage: Perfect; fracture sparry.
Tenacity: Thin plates flexible but inelastic, nonbrittle.
Crystal Form:
Orthorhombic; prismatic to acicular, usually attached, commonly deformed, bladed, radiating fibrous, granular,

massive, compact.
Occurrence: In hydrothermal veins, particularly stibnite-quartz veins, more rarely along with other sulfides in gold, silver, and lead ore veins, rarely metasomatic in limestones.
Associated Minerals: Gold, arsenopyrite, realgar, cinnabar, kermesite.
Similar Minerals:
Bismuthinite is much heavier and more yellowish-white.

2 Argentite, Freiberg (Germany), 4x

3 Bismuthinite, Siegerland (Ger.), 4x

1 Argentite, Freiberg (Saxony, Germany), 4x

1/2 Acanthite/Argentite
Hardness: 2.
Density: 7.3.
Streak: Black, shiny.
Chemical Formula: Ag_2S
Color: Lead-gray; metallic luster, dull tarnish.
Cleavage: Usually indistinct; fracture conchoidal.
Tenacity: Malleable, sectile.
Crystal Form: Above 354°F (179°C), isometric (argentite); below that temperature, monoclinic (acanthite); cubic, octahedral, acicular, massive.
Occurrence: In hydrothermal silver ore veins.
Associated Minerals: Silver,

pyrargyrite.
Similar Minerals: Galena is not malleable; stephanite has a different crystal form.

3 Bismuthinite
Hardness: 2.
Density: 6.8–7.2.
Streak: Gray.
Chemical Formula: Bi_2S_3
Color: Lead-gray to yellowish white, opaque; metallic luster.
Cleavage: Highly perfect; fracture lamellar.
Tenacity: Thin crystals flexible but inelastic, nonbrittle.
Crystal Form:
Orthorhombic; prismatic to

acicular, attached, often embedded, bladed, radiated, massive.
Occurrence: In veins of tin formation and silver-cobalt formation, more rarely in contact deposits and pegmatites.
Associated Minerals: Gold, bismuth, chalcopyrite, arsenopyrite, pyrite.
Similar Minerals: Stibnite is much lighter in weight and somewhat grayer.

5 Jamesonite, Czechoslovakia, 8x

4 Bismuth, Hartenstein (Saxony, Germany), 4x

Crystals of native bismuth are quite rare. Bismuth is obtained mostly from tin, copper, or silver deposits.

4 Bismuth

Hardness: 2–2$^1/_2$.
Density: 9.7–9.8.
Streak: Lead-gray, metallic.
Chemical Formula: Bi
Color: Silver-white with reddish cast, often with darker tarnish; metallic luster.
Cleavage: Perfect, often striated on the cleavage surfaces; fracture hackly to uneven.
Tenacity: Brittle, but sectile.
Crystal Form: Trigonal; crystals rare, massive, lamellar, knitted.
Occurrence: In pegmatites, tin ore veins, hydrothermal veins.

Associated Minerals: Bismuthinite, cassiterite.
Similar Minerals: The low hardness, the color, and the striation on the cleavage surfaces make bismuth unmistakable.

5 Jamesonite

(Feather ore)
Hardness: 2$^1/_2$.
Density: 5.63.
Streak: Dark gray.
Chemical Formula: $Pb_4FeSb_6S_{14}$
Color: Lead-gray; metallic luster.
Cleavage: Rarely discernible.
Tenacity: Brittle.

Crystal Form: Monoclinic; acicular to capillary, tufted.
Occurrence: In hydrothermal ore zones.
Associated Minerals: Sphalerite, arsenopyrite.
Similar Minerals: Jamesonite cannot be distinguished from boulangerite by ordinary methods.

1 Argyrodite, Freiberg (Saxony, Germany), 3x

2 Argyrodite, Bolivia, 4x

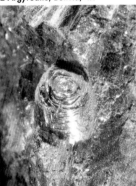

3 Cylindrite, Bolivia, 3x

1/2 Argyrodite
Hardness: 2¹/₂.
Density: 6.2–6.3.
Streak: Grayish black.
Chemical Formula: Ag_8GeS_6
Color: Steel-gray with reddish tone, often with black tarnish; metallic luster.
Cleavage: None; fracture conchoidal.
Tenacity: Brittle.
Crystal Form: Isometric; octahedrons, rhombic dodecahedrons, reniform crusts.
Occurrence: In hydrothermal veins.
Associated Minerals: Argentite, pyrite.

Similar Minerals: Argentite is not brittle.

3 Cylindrite
Hardness: 2¹/₂.
Density: 5.4.
Streak: Dark gray.
Chemical Formula: $Pb_3Sn_4Sb_2S_{12}$
Color: Blackish gray; metallic luster.
Cleavage: None; fracture conchoidal to uneven.
Tenacity: Brittle.
Crystal Form: Uncertain; individuals in the shape of small tubes.
Occurrence: In tin deposits.

Associated Minerals: Cassiterite, franckeite, teallite.
Similar Minerals: The typical development of cylindrite makes any misidentification impossible.

4 Calaverite
Hardness: 2¹/₂.
Density: 9.3.
Streak: Yellowish gray.
Chemical Formula: $AuTe_2$
Color: Silver-white with yellow cast; metallic luster.
Cleavage: None; fracture conchoidal.
Tenacity: Brittle to nonbrittle.
Crystal Form: Monoclinic; prismatic, vertically striated,

4 Calaverite, Colorado, 6x

5 Boulangerite, Trepca
(Yugoslavia), 8x

6 Hessite, Botes (Romania), 8x

large number of faces, often massive.
Occurrence: In hydrothermal veins.
Associated Minerals: Nagyagite, sylvanite, krennerite.
Similar Minerals: Sylvanite, unlike calaverite, has a good cleavage.

5 Boulangerite
Hardness: $2^1/_2$.
Density: 5.8–6.2.
Streak: Black.
Chemical Formula: $Pb_5Sb_4S_{11}$
Color: Lead-gray; metallic luster. In very fine aggre-

gates, silky luster.
Cleavage: None; fracture uneven.
Tenacity: Brittle.
Crystal Form: Monoclinic; acicular to capillary, radiated, fine granular, fibrous, compact.
Occurrence: In lead deposits.
Associated Minerals: Jamesonite cannot be distinguished from boulangerite by ordinary methods.

6 Hessite
Hardness: 2–3.
Density: 8.2–8.4.
Streak: Gray.

Chemical Formula: Ag_2Te
Color: Gray; metallic luster.
Cleavage: Not discernible; fracture uneven.
Tenacity: Sectile.
Crystal Form: Monoclinic; pseudocubic, prismatic, massive, fine granular.
Occurrence: In hydrothermal deposits.
Associated Minerals: Gold.
Similar Minerals: Argentite is hard to distinguish from the much rarer hessite.

2 Chalcocite, Cornwall (England), 2x

1 Stephanite, Freiberg (Saxony, Germany), 8x

3 Semseyite, Romania, 2x

1 Stephanite

Hardness: 2¹/₂.
Density: 6.2–6.3.
Streak: Shiny black.
Chemical Formula:
Ag_5SbS_4
Color: Lead-gray, iron-black, often with black tarnish; metallic luster, dull if tarnished.
Cleavage: Barely discernible; fracture conchoidal to uneven.
Tenacity: Nonbrittle.
Crystal Form:
Orthorhombic; pseudohexagonal through twinning, prismatic, thick tabular, rosette-shaped, rarely massive.

Occurrence: In silver ore veins.
Associated Minerals:
Argentite, polybasite, pyrargyrite.
Similar Minerals: Polybasite is somewhat softer. Argentite has a different crystal form.

2 Chalcocite
(Chalcosine)
Hardness: 2¹/₂–3.
Density: 5.7–5.8.
Streak: Blackish to dark gray, shiny.
Chemical Formula: Cu_2S
Color: Dark lead-gray to blackish; metallic luster, often with dull tarnish.

Cleavage: Not visible; fracture conchoidal.
Tenacity: Nonbrittle.
Crystal Form: Below 217°F (103°C), monoclinic, above that temperature, hexagonal; tabular to prismatic, often massive.
Occurrence: In hydrothermal veins of the cementation zone.
Associated Minerals:
Covellite, enargite, bornite.
Similar Minerals:
Chalcocite is distinguished from other copper sulfides by its tenacity. Digenite is slightly more bluish, but often hard to distinguish.

114

4 Galena, Siegerland (Germany), 2x

5 Galena, Neudorf (Harz Mountains, Germany), 4x

6 Galena, Siegerland (Germany), 4x

Galena is the principal ore of lead.

3 Semseyite
Hardness: $2^1/_2$.
Density: 6.1.
Streak: Black.
Chemical Formula:
$Pb_9Sb_8S_{21}$
Color: Steel-gray; metallic luster.
Cleavage: Perfect; fracture uneven.
Tenacity: Brittle.
Crystal Form: Monoclinic; tabular, often in parallel intergrowths of distorted groups.
Occurrence: In hydrothermal deposits.
Associated Minerals: Pyrite, stibnite.

Similar Minerals: The characteristic aggregate form of semseyite is unmistakable.

4/5/6 Galena
Hardness: $2^1/_2$–3.
Density: 7.2–7.6.
Streak: Dark gray.
Chemical Formula: PbS
Color: Lead-gray; bright metallic luster, often with dull or blue tarnish.
Cleavage: Highly perfect cubic; fracture sparry.
Tenacity: Nonbrittle.
Crystal Form: Isometric; often massive, sometimes attached, usually as cubes, octahedrons, or combinations of the two.
Occurrence: In pegmatites, in high-temperature to low-temperature hydrothermal veins, as replacement in chalks, in sedimentary and resulting metamorphic sulfide deposits.
Associated Minerals: Sphalerite, chalcopyrite, pyrite, barite.
Similar Minerals: Acanthite is much softer and sectile.

2½–3½

Black Streak

1 Bournonite, Georg Mine near Horhausen (Germany), 6x

2 Andorite, Oruro (Bolivia), 3x

Bournonite often forms twinned intergrowths that are reminiscent of cogwheels; the mineral is also popularly known as cogwheel ore.

1 Bournonite
Hardness: 2½–3.
Density: 5.7–5.9.
Streak: Gray.
Chemical Formula:
$PbCuSbS_3$
Color: Steel-gray, lead-gray, iron-black; metallic luster, often with dull tarnish.
Cleavage: Scarcely visible; fracture conchoidal.
Tenacity: Brittle to slightly nonbrittle.
Crystal Form:
Orthorhombic; thick tabular, often massive.
Occurrence: In hydrothermal veins.
Associated Minerals:
Siderite, galena, chalcopyrite, sphalerite.
Similar Minerals:
Tetrahedrite has a different crystal form, but in massive aggregates cannot easily be distinguished from bournonite.

2 Andorite
Hardness: 3–3½.
Density: 5.38.
Streak: Black.
Chemical Formula:
$AgPbSb_3S_6$
Color: Dark steel-gray; metallic luster.
Cleavage: None; fracture conchoidal.
Tenacity: Brittle.
Crystal Form:
Orthorhombic; prismatic, thick tabular, striated along the c axis.
Occurrence: In hydrothermal veins.
Associated Minerals:
Stibnite, cassiterite.
Similar Minerals: The typical crystal form and striation of andorite are characteristic.

3 Bornite
Hardness: 3.
Density: 4.9–5.3.
Streak: Dark gray.
Chemical Formula: Cu_5FeS_4
Color: On fresh break, red-

116

3 Bornite, Morocco, 6x

4 Dyscrasite, Harz Mountains (Germany), 2x

5 Dyscrasite, Pribram (Czechoslovakia), 6x

dish silver-gray with violet cast; colorful tarnish film appears after only a few hours. Metallic luster.
Cleavage: Scarcely visible; fracture conchoidal.
Tenacity: Nonbrittle.
Crystal Form: Above 442°F (228°C), isometric; below that temperature, trigonal or pseudoisometric. Very rarely cubic, usually massive, embedded.
Occurrence: In pegmatites and hydrothermal ore veins, also especially in the cementation zone.
Associated Minerals: Chalcocite, chalcopyrite,

magnetite, gold.
Similar Minerals: The typical tarnish colors distinguish bornite from almost all other sulfides. Tarnished chalcopyrite is always yellow on a fresh fracture surface.

4/5 Dyscrasite
Hardness: $3^1/_2$.
Density: 9.4–10.
Streak: Gray.
Chemical Formula: Ag_3Sb
Color: Silvery white, usually with darker tarnish; metallic luster.
Cleavage: Usually hard to discern; fracture hackly.
Tenacity: Nonbrittle, sectile.

Crystal Form:
Orthorhombic; prismatic, vertically striated, poorly developed, massive.
Occurrence: In hydrothermal silver ore deposits,
Associated Minerals: Native silver and other silver minerals.
Similar Minerals: Argentite/acanthite is softer, and silver does not tarnish; both have quite a different crystal form.

1 Tetrahedrite, Georg Mine (Horhausen, Germany), 6x

2 Moschellandsbergite, Moschellandsberg (Palatinate, Germany), 6x

Mercury often forms compounds with precious metals, so-called amalgams. Many different silver amalgams occur in nature. Moschellandsbergite is by far the most common.

1 Tetrahedrite
Hardness: 3–4.
Density: 4.6–5.2.
Streak: Black.
Chemical Formula: $Cu_3SbS_{3.25}$
Color: Steel-gray to iron-black; metallic luster, but frequently also dull.
Cleavage: None; fracture conchoidal.
Tenacity: Brittle.
Crystal Form: Isometric; usually only tetrahedrons, rarely a greater number of faces, often massive.
Occurrence: Rarely in pegmatites, usually in hydrothermal veins.

Associated Minerals: Pyrite, sphalerite, chalcopyrite, arsenopyrite, galena, silver ores.
Similar Minerals: Sphalerite and galena are distinguished from tetrahedrite by their cleavage. Chalcopyrite is a different color. Tennantite has a somewhat reddish streak when rubbed, but is difficult to distinguish from tetrahedrite by ordinary methods.

2 Moschellandsbergite
(Landsbergite)
Hardness: $3^1/_2$.
Density: 13.7.
Streak: Gray.
Chemical Formula: Ag_2Hg_3
Color: Silvery white; metallic luster.
Cleavage: Not discernible; fracture conchoidal.
Tenacity: Brittle.
Crystal Form: Isometric; rhombic dodecahedrons, globular.
Occurrence: In mercury deposits.
Associated Minerals: Mercury, calomel.
Similar Minerals: Argentite is not brittle.

Black Streak

3 Arsenic, Harz Mountains (Germany), 0.2x

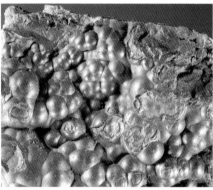

4 Chalcopyrite, Cornwall (England), 2x

Chalcopyrite is the chief copper ore, as well as the most common. An ore deposit that contains even relatively tiny amounts of chalcopyrite is thus an economically mineable copper deposit.

5 Chalcopyrite, Siegerland (Germany), 3x

3 Arsenic
Hardness: 3–4.
Density: 7.06.
Streak: Black.
Chemical Formula: As
Color: Dark gray to black; on fresh surface, metallic luster, quickly tarnishing to dark and dull.
Cleavage: Not visible; fracture uneven.
Tenacity: Brittle.
Crystal Form: Trigonal; rarely pseudocubic to acicular crystals, usually shelly, resembling limonite, radiated, compact.
Occurrence: In arsenic-bearing silver and cobalt ore veins.

Associated Minerals: Native silver, dyscrasite.
Similar Minerals: Reniform pyrite and marcasite are harder. Goethite has a different streak.

4/5 Chalcopyrite
Hardness: $3^{1}/_{2}$–4.
Density: 4.2–4.3.
Streak: Dark green.
Chemical Formula: $CuFeS_2$
Color: Brass-yellow with greenish cast, often with iridescent tarnish. Metallic luster.
Cleavage: Scarcely discernible; fracture conchoidal.
Tenacity: Brittle.

Crystal Form: Tetragonal; pseudotetrahedral crystals, usually massive.
Occurrence: In granites and gabbros, in pegmatites and tin ore veins, in hydrothermal veins and black schists.
Associated Minerals: Pyrite, sphalerite, pyrrhotite, tetrahedrite, fluorite.
Similar Minerals: Pyrite is harder. Pyrrhotite is more brown in color. Gold is softer and sectile.

Black Streak

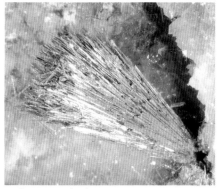

1 Millerite, Siegerland (Germany), 4x

2 Millerite, Siegerland (Germany), 3x

3 Cubanite, Harz Mountains (Germany), 8x

Because it commonly occurs in capillary crystals, the nickel sulfide millerite also is called capillary pyrites.

1/2 Millerite
(Capillary pyrites)
Hardness: 3¹/₂.
Density: 5.3.
Streak: Dark green.
Chemical Formula: NiS
Color: Brass-yellow; metallic luster.
Cleavage: Perfect, but almost never discernible because of the acicular development; fracture uneven.
Tenacity: Brittle.
Crystal Form: Trigonal; acicular, usually capillary, very rarely massive.
Occurrence: In nickel deposits, as alteration product of other nickel ores.

Associated Minerals: Gersdorffite, bravoite, calcite.
Similar Minerals: The typical development and the color preclude any misidentification.

3 Cubanite
Hardness: 3¹/₂–4.
Density: 4.10.
Streak: Black.
Chemical Formula: $CuFe_2S_3$
Color: Bronze-yellow; metallic luster.
Cleavage: Usually not discernible; fracture conchoidal.
Tenacity: Brittle.
Crystal Form: Orthorhombic; prismatic, longitudinally striated, but generally massive.
Occurrence: Intergrown with chalcopyrite in lamellar fashion in almost all relatively high-temperature copper deposits.
Associated Minerals: Chalcopyrite, pyrrhotite, siderite.
Similar Minerals: The fine intergrowths with chalcopyrite are not distinguishable by ordinary methods. Cubanite crystals are distinguished from elongated pyrite crystals by darker color and longitudinal striation.

4 Tennantite, Turkey, 10x

Tennantite and tetrahedrite, two isostructural fahlores, sometimes contain substantial amounts of silver, in which case they are major silver ores.

5 Enargite, Butte, Montana, 6x

4 Tennantite

Hardness: 3–4.
Density: 4.6–5.2.
Streak: Black, brownish red when rubbed.
Chemical Formula: $Cu_3AsS_{3.25}$
Color: Steel-gray, translucent reddish in very thin splinters; metallic luster, often dull.
Cleavage: None; fracture conchoidal.
Tenacity: Brittle.
Crystal Form: Isometric; tetrahedral, granular, massive.
Occurrence: In hydrothermal veins.
Associated Minerals: Pyrite, chalcopyrite, arsenopyrite.

Similar Minerals:
Arsenopyrite is harder. Galena has an excellent cleavage. Tetrahedrite is somewhat lighter in color and its streak is not reddish when rubbed. Enargite has a perfect cleavage.

5 Enargite

Hardness: 3¹/₂.
Density: 4.4.
Streak: Black.
Chemical Formula: Cu_3AsS_4
Color: Steel-gray to iron-black with violet cast; metallic luster.
Cleavage: Perfect prismatic; fracture uneven.
Tenacity: Brittle.
Crystal Form:
Orthorhombic, pseudohexagonal; prismatic, radiated, granular, massive.
Occurrence: In arsenic-containing copper ore veins.
Associated Minerals:
Tennantite, chalcocite.
Similar Minerals:
Arsenopyrite is harder. Tetrahedrite has a different crystal form and no cleavage.

121

1 Pyrrhotite, Harz Mountains (Germany), 6x

3 Siegenite, Siegerland (Germany), 4x

2 Pyrrhotite, Russia, 0.5x

The mineral siegenite was named for the town of Siegen in the Siegerland (Germany). This generally rare mineral has since been found in American deposits as well, but the best and most famous specimens still come from the Siegerland.

1/2 Pyrrhotite

Hardness: 4.
Density: 4.6.
Streak: Dark gray.
Chemical Formula: FeS
Color: Bronze with brownish cast (tombac color); metallic luster.
Cleavage: Rarely visible; fracture uneven.
Tenacity: Brittle.
Crystal Form: Hexagonal; rarely prismatic to tabular, usually massive.
Occurrence: In hydrothermal veins and metamorphic pyrite deposits.
Associated Minerals: Pyrite, pentlandite, sphalerite, chalcopyrite.
Special Property: Pyrrhotite is attracted by magnets and deviates the compass needle.
Similar Minerals: Pyrite and chalcopyrite are much yellower. Pyrite, moreover, is harder. Sphalerite has a perfect cleavage.

3 Siegenite

Hardness: 4¹/₂–5¹/₂.
Density: 4.5–4.8.
Streak: Gray.
Chemical Formula: $(Co,Ni)_3S_4$
Color: Steel-gray, silvery, often with brownish tarnish; metallic luster.
Cleavage: Not discernible; fracture uneven.
Tenacity: Brittle.
Crystal Form: Isometric; octahedrons, often intergrown in botryoidal shapes.
Occurrence: In hydrothermal deposits.
Associated Minerals: Chalcopyrite, pyrite.
Similar Minerals: This mineral is characterized by its brownish tarnish. Pyrite is much more yellowish. Galena has perfect cleavage.

4 Iron, Russia, 0.5x

5 Platinum, Urals (Russia), 2x

Native iron that—like the iron shown here—originated on earth is called terrestrial iron. Unlike meteoric iron, which came to us from space, it is extremely rare.

4 Iron
Hardness: 4–5.
Density: 7.88.
Streak: Steel-gray, shiny.
Chemical Formula: Fe. Nickel is abundant in meteoric iron.
Color: Steel-gray to iron-black; metallic luster.
Cleavage: None; fracture hackly.
Tenacity: Malleable.
Crystal Form: Isometric; small scales, drops, irregular masses.
Occurrence: In basalts and meteorites.
Associated Minerals: Wuestite, olivine, taenite, schreibersite.
Special Property: Iron is attracted by magnets and deviates the compass needle.
Similar Minerals: The paragenesis and tenacity of iron make misidentification impossible.

5 Platinum
Hardness: 4–4¹/₂.
Density: 21.4.
Streak: Gray.
Chemical Formula: Pt
Color: Silver-gray; metallic luster.
Cleavage: None; fracture hackly.
Tenacity: Ductile, malleable.
Crystal Form: Isometric; cubic, rounded nuggets, thin plates.
Occurrence: In placers and quartz veins.
Associated Minerals: Gold, chromite.
Similar Minerals: Silver is softer. Iron is magnetic.

1 Hollandite, Norway, 2x

2 Safflorite, Schneeberg (Germany), 4x

When safflorite is slightly weathered on the surface, it is distinguished from the similar nickel and iron minerals by its pink weathering crust.

1 Hollandite
Hardness: 6.
Density: 4.95.
Streak: Black.
Chemical Formula: $Ba(Mn,Fe)_8O_{16}$
Color: Black, blackish brown; metallic luster to dull.
Cleavage: Poor; fracture uneven.
Tenacity: Brittle.
Crystal Form: Monoclinic; prismatic, fibrous, reniform, massive.
Occurrence: In manganese deposits.
Associated Minerals: Other manganese oxides.
Similar Minerals: Psilomelane is indistinguishable from hollandite by ordinary methods.

2 Safflorite
Hardness: 4¹/₂–5¹/₂.
Density: 6.9–7.3.
Streak: Black.
Chemical Formula: $CoAs_2$
Color: Tin-white, rapidly darkening when exposed to air; metallic luster.
Cleavage: Scarcely visible; fracture conchoidal.
Tenacity: Brittle.
Crystal Form: Monoclinic; crystals very small, tabular, often intergrown to form star-shaped trillings, massive.
Occurrence: In hydrothermal cobalt-nickel-silver veins.
Associated Minerals: Native arsenic, calcite, erythrite.
Similar Minerals: Arsenopyrite is harder. Chloanthite and skutterudite have a different crystal form. Loellingite is indistinguishable by ordinary methods, although the presence of the weathering residue erythrite can be indicative.

4 Maucherite, Harz Mountains (Germany), 6x

3 Carrollite, Shaba (Zaire), 8x

Maucherite was named for Professor Maucher of Munich, a famous mineralogist and specialist in the study of mineral deposits.

3 Carrollite
Hardness: $4^1/_2$–$5^1/_2$.
Density: 4.5–4.8.
Streak: Gray.
Chemical Formula: $CuCo_2S_4$
Color: Light gray to steel-gray; metallic luster.
Cleavage: Poor; fracture conchoidal.
Tenacity: Brittle.
Crystal Form: Isometric; octahedrons, massive.
Occurrence: In hydrothermal deposits.
Associated Minerals: Calcite, pyrite.
Similar Minerals: Carrollite is difficult to distinguish from linneite by ordinary methods.

4 Maucherite:
Hardness: 5–6.
Density: 8.0.
Streak: Brownish to blackish.
Chemical Formula: $Ni_{11}As_8$
Color: Reddish silver-white, often with darker tarnish; metallic luster.
Cleavage: None; fracture conchoidal.
Tenacity: Brittle.
Crystal Form: Tetragonal; rarely tabular, whorled, lamellar, bladed, massive.
Occurrence: In cobalt-nickel-arsenic veins.
Associated Minerals: Niccolite, calcite, cobaltite, chloanthite.
Similar Minerals: Niccolite has more prismatic crystals and in the massive state is indistinguishable from maucherite by ordinary methods. The other cobalt and nickel minerals, such as chloanthite, rammelsbergite, skutterudite, cobaltite, and safflorite, are always distinctly silvery white or gray; this color distinguishes them clearly from maucherite, which is reddish.

1 Ilmenite, Froland (Norway), 3x

2 Cobaltite, Siegerland
(Germany), 4x

The black streak distinguishes ilmenite from hematite, which is similar but has a red streak.

1 Ilmenite

Hardness: 5–6.
Density: 4.5–5.0.
Streak: Black.
Chemical Formula: $FeTiO_3$
Color: Iron-black; metallic luster, but often with dull tarnish.
Cleavage: None; fracture conchoidal to uneven.
Tenacity: Brittle.
Crystal Form: Trigonal; rhombohedral, thick to thin tabular, granular, massive.
Occurrence: In igneous rocks, pegmatites, placers.
Associated Minerals: Hematite, magnetite, rutile, apatite.

Similar Minerals: Magnetite has a different crystal form. Hematite has a different streak.

2 Cobaltite

Hardness: $5^1/_2$.
Density: 6.0–6.4.
Streak: Dark gray.
Chemical Formula: CoAsS
Color: Silver-white with reddish cast; metallic luster.
Cleavage: Scarcely visible; fracture conchoidal.
Tenacity: Brittle.
Crystal Form: Isometric; cubes, often striated, octahedrons and rhombic dodecahedrons, often embedded, massive.
Occurrence: In hydrothermal veins, regional metamorphic deposits.
Associated Minerals: Chalcopyrite, pyrite, skutterudite, chloanthite.
Similar Minerals: Efflorescences of erythrite make differentiation from the nickel ores easier.

3/5 Allanite
(Orthite)
Hardness: $5^1/_2$.
Density: 3.0–4.2.
Streak: Greenish gray to dark brown.

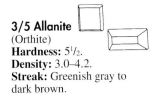

3 Allanite, Spain, 4x

4 Loellingite, Australia, 4x

5 Allanite, New Mexico, 6x

Chemical Formula:
Ca(Ce,Th)(Fe,Mg)Al$_2$
[O/OH/SiO$_4$/Si$_2$O$_7$]
Color: Pitch-black when
opaque; brownish or violet-
brown when translucent.
Greasy vitreous luster.
Cleavage: Not discernible;
fracture conchoidal.
Tenacity: Brittle.
Crystal Form: Monoclinic;
rarely tabular, acicular, often
massive and embedded.
Occurrence: In granites,
syenites, diorites, gneisses,
pegmatites, pyroclasts.
Associated Minerals:
Monazite, xenotime, feldspar,
quartz.

Similar Minerals: Black
tourmaline is harder. Rutile
never has any kind of violet
tone or cast.

4 Loellingite
Hardness: 5–6.
Density: 7.1–7.4.
Streak: Dark gray.
Chemical Formula: FeAs$_2$
Color: Silver-white, tarnish-
ing to darker color; metallic
luster.
Cleavage: Discernible basal;
fracture uneven.
Tenacity: Brittle.
Crystal Form:
Orthorhombic; acicular,
prismatic, tabular, often star-

shaped trillings, bladed,
radiated, granular, embedded.
Occurrence: In tin ore veins,
pegmatites, hydrothermal
veins.
Associated Minerals:
Siderite, arsenopyrite.
Similar Minerals:
Arsenopyrite is lighter in
weight, somewhat harder,
and slightly darker on a fresh
surface. Safflorite is indistinguishable from loellingite by
ordinary methods, but the
frequent efflorescence of
erythrite is indicative.

127

1 Arsenopyrite, Panasqueira (Portugal), 4x

2 Arsenopyrite, Korea, 8x

3 Columbite, Portugal, 2x

1/2 Arsenopyrite
Hardness: 5¹/₂–6.
Density: 5.9–6.2.
Streak: Black.
Chemical Formula: FeAsS
Color: Tin-white to steel-gray, often with darker tarnish; metallic luster.
Cleavage: Indistinct; fracture uneven.
Tenacity: Brittle.
Crystal Form: Orthorhombic; pseudo-octahedral to prismatic, often twins, some of which are star-shaped, massive.
Occurrence: In tin ore veins and hydrothermal veins.
Associated Minerals: Pyrite, gold, pyrrhotite, siderite, chalcopyrite.
Similar Minerals: Pyrite and marcasite are a different color. Pyrrhotite is slightly softer. Loellingite is somewhat heavier and softer.

3 Columbite
Hardness: 6.
Density: 5.3–8.1.
Streak: Brown to black.
Chemical Formula: The columbites are members of a solid solution series of niobite $(Fe,Mn)Nb_2O_6$ and tantalite $(Fe,Mn)Ta_2O_6$.
Color: Brownish black to black; pitchy luster.
Cleavage: Barely visible; fracture conchoidal.
Tenacity: Brittle.
Crystal Form: Orthorhombic; tabular to acicular, radiated, embedded.
Occurrence: In pegmatites.
Associated Minerals: Uraninite, quartz, feldspar.
Similar Minerals: Hematite has a different streak. Ilmenite has a different crystal form.

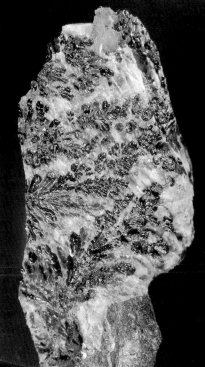

4 Ilvaite, Serifos (Greece), 2x

5 Uraninite, Saxony (Germany), 2x

4 Ilvaite

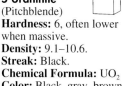

Hardness: 5¹/₂–6.
Density: 4.1.
Streak: Blackish.
Chemical Formula:
$CaFe_2^{+2}Fe^{+3}[OH/O/Si_2O_7]$
Color: Black; vitreous luster, somewhat resinous, dull.
Cleavage: Barely discernible; fracture conchoidal.
Tenacity: Brittle.
Crystal Form:
Orthorhombic; prismatic, radiated, bladed, granular, massive.
Occurrence: In contact deposits where iron is abundant.
Associated Minerals: Hedenbergite, magnetite, pyrite, hematite, arsenopyrite.
Similar Minerals:
Tourmaline is harder. Actinolite has a different paragenesis and cleavage.

5 Uraninite
(Pitchblende)
Hardness: 6, often lower when massive.
Density: 9.1–10.6.
Streak: Black.
Chemical Formula: UO_2
Color: Black, gray, brownish; greasy luster, often dull.
Cleavage: Usually not visible; fracture conchoidal.
Tenacity: Brittle.
Crystal Form: Isometric; cubes, octahedrons, reniform, botryoidal, earthy, massive.
Occurrence: In pegmatites, in microscopic form in granites, in hydrothermal veins, in sandstones and Precambrian placers.
Associated Minerals: Uranyl phosphate ores, uranophane.
Special Property: Uraninite is highly radioactive.
Similar Minerals: Magnetite has a different luster, is magnetic, and is not radioactive.

129

1 Ullmannite, Siegerland (Ger.), 4x

2 Rammelsbergite, Morocco, 4x

3 Skutterudite, Schneeberg (Germany), 6x

1 Ullmannite

Hardness: 5–5¹/₂.
Density: 6.65.
Streak: Black.
Chemical Formula: NiSbS
Color: Steel-gray; metallic luster.
Cleavage: Perfect; fracture uneven.
Tenacity: Brittle.
Crystal Form: Isometric; cubes, octahedrons, massive.
Occurrence: In hydrothermal veins.
Associated Minerals: Siderite, linneite.
Similar Minerals: Almost indistinguishable from gersdorffite.

2 Rammelsbergite
Hardness: 5¹/₂–6.
Density: 6.97.
Streak: Gray.
Chemical Formula: $NiAs_2$
Color: Tin-white with reddish cast, usually with yellow tarnish; metallic luster.
Cleavage: None; fracture uneven.
Tenacity: Brittle.
Crystal Form: Orthorhombic; tabular, often intergrown in cockscomb shapes.
Occurrence: In hydrothermal deposits.
Associated Minerals: Skutterudite, loellingite.

Similar Minerals:
Loellingite in crystals is indistinguishable from rammelsbergite by ordinary methods, but the paragenesis gives unmistakable clues.

3 Skutterudite
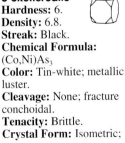

Hardness: 6.
Density: 6.8.
Streak: Black.
Chemical Formula: $(Co,Ni)As_3$
Color: Tin-white; metallic luster.
Cleavage: None; fracture conchoidal.
Tenacity: Brittle.
Crystal Form: Isometric;

4 Pyrite, Habachtal (Austria), 2x

5 Pyrite, Siegerland (Germany), 1x

6 Pyrite, Poona (India), 4x

7 Pyrite, Huanzala (Peru), 1x

octahedral crystals, often massive.
Occurrence: In cobalt-nickel deposits.
Associated Minerals: Chloanthite, cobaltite.
Similar Minerals: Chloanthite is indistinguishable from skutterudite by ordinary methods. Coats of erythrite or annabergite provide clues. Safflorite has a different crystal form.

4/5/6/7 Pyrite
Hardness: 6–6½.
Density: 5.0–5.2.
Streak: Dark green.
Chemical Formula: FeS_2
Color: Light brass-yellow; metallic luster.
Cleavage: None; fracture conchoidal.
Tenacity: Brittle.
Crystal Form: Isometric; cubes with striated faces, octahedrons, pentagonal dodecahedrons, radiating fibrous, reniform, often also massive.
Occurrence: In rocks, intramagmatic deposits, hydrothermal veins, as

concretion in sediments, in metamorphic deposits.
Associated Minerals: Sphalerite, galena, quartz, calcite.
Similar Minerals: Marcasite has a different crystal form and is distinctly more greenish, but when massive, reniform, or radiated it often is indistinguishable by ordinary methods. Chalcopyrite is softer.

131

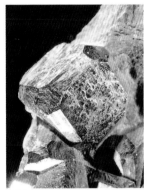

1 Chloanthite, Schneeberg (Ger.), 3x

3 Pyrolusite, Harz Mountains (Germany), 1x

2 Pyrolusite, Siegerland (Ger.), 2x

1 Chloanthite

(Nickel-skutterudite)
Hardness: 5½.
Density: 6.4–6.6.
Streak: Dark-gray.
Chemical Formula:
$(Ni,Co)As_3$
Color: Tin-white, often with darker tarnish; metallic luster.
Cleavage: None; fracture uneven.
Tenacity: Brittle.
Crystal Form: Isometric; cubic, granular, massive, embedded.
Occurrence: In hydrothermal cobalt-nickel deposits.
Associated Minerals:
Safflorite, skutterudite,
arsenic.
Similar Minerals:
Skutterudite is indistinguishable from chloanthite by ordinary methods. Coats of annabergite clearly suggest chloanthite, however. Safflorite and rammelsbergite are slightly softer and heavier, and they have a different crystal form.

2/3 Pyrolusite

Hardness: 6, but in aggregates often much lower.
Density: 4.9–5.1.
Streak: Black.
Chemical Formula: MnO_2
Color: Silver-gray to flat black; metallic luster to dull.
Cleavage: None; fracture conchoidal, in aggregates crumbly to fibrous.
Tenacity: Brittle.
Crystal Form: Tetragonal; prismatic, radiating fibrous, earthy, crusty.
Occurrence: In hydrothermal veins, in the oxidation zone, in sediments as oolites.

4 Magnetite, Pakistan, 10x

Massive specimens of magnetite can be strongly magnetic and capable of attracting small pieces of iron, nails, or needles.

5 Magnetite, Stubachtal (Austria), 2x

Associated Minerals: Manganite, psilomelane, limonite.
Similar Minerals: Manganite has a brown streak. Antimonite is less brittle and much softer.

4/5 Magnetite
Hardness: 6–6½.
Density: 5.2.
Streak: Black.
Chemical Formula: Fe_3O_4
Color: Iron-black; dull metallic luster.
Cleavage: Barely discernible; fracture conchoidal.
Tenacity: Brittle.

Crystal Form: Isometric; octahedrons, rhombic dodecahedrons, attached and embedded, massive.
Occurrence: In igneous rocks, pneumatolytic replacement deposits, metamorphic deposits, embedded in chlorite and talc schists, in hydrothermal veins.
Associated Minerals: Pyrite, ilmenite, hematite, apatite.
Special Property: Magnetite is magnetic. It deviates the magnetic compass needle and is attracted by magnets. Massive magnetite specimens themselves can attract iron filings, needles, nails, or

other small bits of iron.
Similar Minerals: All similar minerals are either non-magnetic or only slightly magnetic. Chromite has a light-brown streak.

133

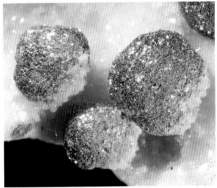

1 Marcasite, Sauerland (Germany), 3x

3 Bixbyite, Utah, 4x

2 Marcasite, Westphalia (Germany), 2x

Radiating fibrous pyrite is frequently called marcasite, but this aggregate form is not especially characteristic of marcasite.

1/2 Marcasite

Hardness: 6–6¹/₂.
Density: 4.8–4.9.
Streak: Greenish black.
Chemical Formula: FeS_2
Color: Brass-yellow with green cast; metallic luster.
Cleavage: Poor; fracture uneven.
Tenacity: Brittle.
Crystal Form: Orthorhombic; tabular, radiated, lamellated, reniform, massive.
Occurrence: In replacement deposits, as concretion.
Associated Minerals: Pyrite, pyrrhotite.
Similar Minerals: Pyrite

lacks a greenish cast and has a different crystal form. Chalcopyrite is softer. Pyrrhotite and arsenopyrite are a different color.

3 Bixbyite

Hardness: 6¹/₂.
Density: 4.9–5.0.
Streak: Black.
Chemical Formula: $(Mn,Fe)_2O_3$
Color: Black; metallic luster.
Cleavage: Discernible octahedral; fracture uneven.
Tenacity: Brittle.
Crystal Form: Isometric; cubic, often massive.
Occurrence: In metamorphic manganese deposits; in volcanic rocks and their cavities.
Associated Minerals: Topaz, spessartine, braunite, hausmannite.
Similar Minerals: Magnetite lacks cleavage and almost never forms cubes.

4 Romanechite, Saxony (Germany), 1x

6 Epidote, Riveo (Ticino, Switzerland), 2x

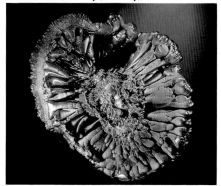

5 Romanechite, Siegerland (Germany), 1x

7 Epidote, Habachtal (Austria), 2x

4/5 Romanechite
(Psilomelane)
Hardness: 6–6$\frac{1}{2}$; variable, depending on aggregate form.
Density: 6.3–6.45.
Streak: Dark brown.
Chemical Formula: $BaMn_8O_{16}(OH)_4$
Color: Black to steel-gray; metallic luster to dull.
Cleavage: None; fracture uneven.
Tenacity: Brittle.
Crystal Form: Monoclinic; reniform, stalactitic, radiated, massive.
Occurrence: In weathering deposits, as concretions in sediments, as replacements in chalks.
Associated Minerals: Other manganese oxides.
Similar Minerals: Pyrolusite has a different crystal form, but when massive or in reniform aggregates it is quite difficult to distinguish.

6/7 Epidote
Hardness: 6–7.
Density: 3.3–3.5.
Streak: Gray.
Chemical Formula: $Ca_2(Fe,Al)Al_2[O/OH/SiO_4/Si_2O_7]$
Color: Yellowish green, dark green; vitreous luster.
Cleavage: Not prominent; fracture conchoidal.
Tenacity: Brittle.
Crystal Form: Monoclinic; prismatic, rarely thick tabular, radiated, massive.
Occurrence: In pegmatites, in epidote schists, lining fissures of granites and metamorphic rocks.
Associated Minerals: Actinolite, diopside, albite, apatite.
Similar Minerals: Augite, hornblende, and actinolite have perfect cleavage. Tourmaline has a different crystal form.

135

White

Minerals with a white to
extremely pale streak are
grouped here.
   Minerals that are harder than
the porcelain of the streak plate
(about 6 on the Mohs hardness
scale) merely raise white powder
from the streak-plate material
when you try to perform a streak
test. Because such borderline
cases are difficult to determine,
these minerals are also included
in this group.

Pyromorphite crystals, so-called
Emser barrels, from Bad Ems
(Germany). Size of these crystals is
up to about $^3/_4$ inches (2 cm).

1 Mercury, Spain, 6x

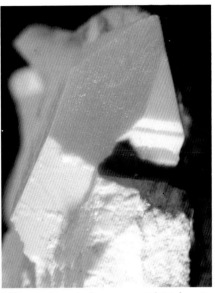

3 Talc pseudomorph after quartz crystal, Göpfersgrün (Fichtelgebirge, Germany), 6x

The pseudomorphs of talc after quartz can easily be recognized by the fact that they have the crystal form of hard quartz, but can be scratched by a fingernail.

2 Talc, Carinthia (Austria), 2x

1 Mercury
Hardness: —
Density: 13.6.
Streak: White.
Chemical Formula: Hg
Color: Tin-white; metallic luster.
Cleavage: None.
Crystal Form: Liquid, forms droplets.
Occurrence: In mercury deposits.
Associated Minerals: Cinnabar, schwatzite.
Similar Minerals: As the only liquid mineral, mercury is unmistakable.

2/3 Talc
(Steatite, Soapstone)
Hardness: 1.
Density: 2.7–2.8.
Streak: White.
Chemical Formula: $Mg_3[(OH)_2/Si_4O_{10}]$
Color: White, gray, yellow, brown, green; pearly to greasy luster.
Cleavage: Perfect basal; fracture uneven to lamellar.
Tenacity: Flexible, nonbrittle.
Crystal Form: Monoclinic; lamellar, compact with reniform surface; often pseudomorphs after other minerals.
Occurrence: In metamorphic rocks, as talc schist, potstone (steatite); foliated aggregates as cavity fillings in serpentines.
Associated Minerals: Dolomite, magnesite, serpentine.
Similar Minerals: The softness and the greasy feel make talc fairly unmistakable.

4 Larderellite
Hardness: 1.
Density: 1.90.
Streak: White.
Chemical Formula: $NH_4B_5O_6(OH)_4$
Color: White; dull.
Cleavage: Perfect; fracture uneven.

4 Larderellite, Italy, 4x

5 Leiteite, Tsumeb (Namibia), 1x

6 Glaucokerinite, Lavrion (Greece), 3x

Tenacity: Nonbrittle.
Crystal Form: Monoclinic; crusty.
Occurrence: As deposit of boron-containing waters.
Associated Minerals: Other boron minerals.
Similar Minerals: None.

5 Leiteite
Hardness: 1¹/₂.
Density: 4.3.
Streak: White.
Chemical Formula: $(Zn,Fe)As_2O_4$
Color: White, pink; pearly luster.
Cleavage: Perfect; fracture lamellar.

Tenacity: Nonbrittle.
Crystal Form: Monoclinic; lamellar cleavage fragments.
Occurrence: In the oxidation zone.
Associated Minerals: Schneiderhoehnite, scorodite.
Similar Minerals: The high density, tenacity, and cleavage make leiteite unmistakable.

6 Glaucokerinite
Hardness: 1.
Density: 2.75.
Streak: White.
Chemical Formula: $(Zn,Cu)_{10}Al_4SO_4(OH)_{30} \cdot 2H_2O$
Color: White to blue; dull.

Cleavage: Not discernible; fracture uneven.
Tenacity: Nonbrittle.
Crystal Form: Monoclinic; crusty, compact with reniform surface, radiating fibrous.
Occurrence: In the oxidation zone.
Associated Minerals: Azurite, adamite.
Similar Minerals: Glaucokerinite is unmistakable.

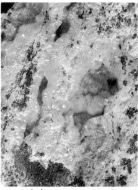

2 Aurichalcite, Saxony (Ger.), 2x

1 Sal ammoniac, Tadzhikistan, 2x

The sal ammoniac crystals pictured here come from a cave in a region of burning coal seams, discovered by Alexander the Great on his expedition of conquest.

1 Sal ammoniac
Hardness: 1–2.
Density: 1.52.
Streak: White.
Chemical Formula: NH_4Cl
Color: White; dull.
Cleavage: Not discernible; fracture earthy.
Tenacity: Brittle.
Crystal Form: Isometric; earthy, crusty.
Occurrence: On volcanic rocks and burning coal.
Associated Minerals: Sulfur, alum.
Similar Minerals: Alum is indistinguishable by ordinary methods.

2 Aurichalcite
Hardness: 2.
Density: 3.6–4.3
Streak: White to light-blue.
Chemical Formula:
$(Zn,Cu)_5[(OH)_3/CO_3]_2$
Color: Light blue, bluish, greenish blue; silky to pearly luster.
Cleavage: Perfect; fracture micaceous.
Tenacity: Nonbrittle.
Crystal Form: Orthorhombic; lamellar, acicular, radiating fibrous, in tufts.
Occurrence: Oxidation zone.
Associated Minerals: Hemimorphite, smithsonite, rosasite.
Special Property: Effervesces with dilute HCl.
Similar Minerals: Rosasite is harder and never lamellar; serpierite is harder and does not effervesce with dilute hydrochloric acid.

3/4 Chlorargyrite
(Cerargyrite, Horn silver)
Hardness: $1^1/_2$.
Density: 5.5–5.6.
Streak: White to gray; shiny.
Chemical Formula: AgCl
Color: Colorless, white, yellowish, brownish, gray, black; adamantine to greasy

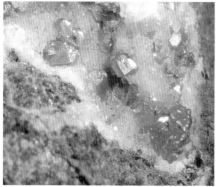

3 Chlorargyrite, Chile, 4x

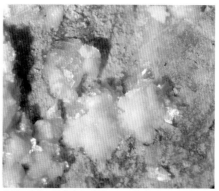

5 Guerinite, Richelsdorf (Germany), 6x

4 Chlorargyrite, Harz Mountains (Germany), 3x

6 Pyrophyllite, California, 2x

luster.
Cleavage: None; fracture hackly.
Tenacity: Ductile, sectile.
Crystal Form: Isometric; rarely cubic crystals, usually crusty, reniform, massive.
Occurrence: Oxidation zone.
Associated Minerals: Argentite, native silver.
Similar Minerals: The color, luster, and tenacity are characteristic.

5 Guerinite
Hardness: 1¹/₂.
Density: 2.68.
Streak: White.

Chemical Formula: $Ca_5H_2(AsO_4)_4 \cdot 9H_2O$
Color: White; pearly luster.
Cleavage: Perfect; fracture fibrous.
Tenacity: Brittle.
Crystal Form: Monoclinic; tabular, acicular.
Occurrence: Oxidation zone.
Associated Minerals: Pharmacolite, picropharmacolite.
Similar Minerals: Picropharmacolite has a different crystal form.

6 Pyrophyllite
Hardness: 1¹/₂.

Density: 2.8.
Streak: White.
Chemical Formula: $(Al_2[(OH)_2/Si_4O_{10}]$
Color: White, yellow, green, brown; pearly luster.
Cleavage: Perfect; fracture uneven.
Tenacity: Flexible, nonbrittle.
Crystal Form: Monoclinic; lamellar, radiating fibrous, compact.
Occurrence: In schists, as lining in ore veins.
Associated Minerals: Quartz.
Similar Minerals: Talc is indistinguishable by ordinary methods.

2 Annabergite, Lavrion (Greece), 3x

1 Vivianite, Kerch (Ukraine), 2x

Vivianite commonly occurs in cavities in fossils such as shells and snails, or on fossil bones.

1 Vivianite
Hardness: 2.
Density: 2.6–2.7.
Streak: White to faintly light blue.
Chemical Formula:
$Fe_3[PO_4]2 \cdot 8H_2O$
Color: Green to blue; pearly luster.
Cleavage: Perfect; fracture lamellar.
Tenacity: Flexible in thin sheets, nonbrittle.
Crystal Form: Monoclinic; prismatic to tabular, globular, massive, powdery, earthy, as crusts.
Occurrence: In pegmatites, in the oxidation zone, in sediments.
Associated Minerals: Triphylite, siderite, limonite.
Similar Minerals: Azurite effervesces with dilute hydrochloric acid. Lazulite has a greasy luster and is harder.

2 Annabergite
Hardness: 2.
Density: 3.0–3.1.
Streak: White.
Chemical Formula:
$Ni_3[AsO_4]_2 \cdot 8H_2O$
Color: Light green to apple-green; vitreous luster.
Cleavage: Highly perfect; fracture lamellar.
Tenacity: Nonbrittle, flexible in thin sheets.
Crystal Form: Monoclinic; prismatic to tabular, acicular, usually massive, earthy, crusty.
Occurrence: In the oxidation zone.
Associated Minerals: Nickel ores.
Similar Minerals: Malachite and other green copper minerals are darker; malachite effervesces with dilute hydrochloric acid.

White Streak

3 Autunite, Bergen (Vogtland, Germany), 2x

4 Autunite, Bergen (Germany), 2x

5 Thomsenolite, Greenland, 6x

3/4 Autunite
Hardness: 2–2¹/₂.
Density: 3.2.
Streak: White to yellowish.
Chemical Formula:
$Ca[UO_2/PO_4]_2 \cdot 8–12H_2O$
Color: Yellow with green cast. Vitreous luster; pearly luster on cleavage surfaces.
Cleavage: Perfect basal; fracture uneven.
Tenacity: Brittle to nonbrittle.
Crystal Form: Tetragonal; tabular, scaly.
Occurrence: In the oxidation zone, as lining in fissures.
Associated Minerals: Torbernite, uraninite.
Special Property: Autunite fluoresces and is radioactive!
Similar Minerals: Torbernite is green and not fluorescent. Uranocircite has a more yellowish streak.

5 Thomsenolite
Hardness: 2.
Density: 2.98.
Streak: White.
Chemical Formula: $CaNaAlF_6 \cdot H_2O$
Color: Colorless, white, yellowish, brownish because of limonite; vitreous luster.
Cleavage: Perfect; fracture uneven.
Tenacity: Brittle.
Crystal Form: Monoclinic; long to short prismatic, commonly striated crosswise.
Occurrence: In druses in decomposed cryolite.
Associated Minerals: Pachnolite, ralstonite, cryolite.
Similar Minerals: Pachnolite crystals are rhomboid in cross section and lack horizontal striations. Ralstonite is harder and has a different crystal form.

143

2 Parasymplesite, Alsace (Fr.), 10x

Many of the large sulfur deposits resulted from the activity of sulfate-reducing bacteria.

1 Sulfur, Agrigento (Sicily, Italy), 2x

1 Sulfur

Hardness: 2.
Density: 2.0–2.1.
Streak: White.
Chemical Formula: S
Color: Yellow, brownish yellow, greenish yellow, transparent to opaque; resinous to greasy luster, adamantine luster on crystal faces.
Cleavage: Virtually absent; fracture conchoidal.
Tenacity: Very brittle.
Crystal Form: Orthorhombic; bipyramids common, steep pyramidal, rarely tabular, attached, granular, fibrous, reniform, stalactitic, earthy, powdery.
Occurrence: Near volcanic gas outbursts, veins, beds, nests, impregnations in sedimentary rocks, in salt deposits, lining ore deposits with sulfidic ores, as a filling in fossil cavities, coating druses in marbles.
Associated Minerals: Calcite, celestite, aragonite, sulfides.
Similar Minerals: The rare yellow sphalerite is readily distinguishable from sulfur by its good cleavage.

2 Parasymplesite

Hardness: 2.
Density: 3.1.
Streak: White.
Chemical Formula: $Fe_3(AsO_4)_2 \cdot 8H_2O$
Color: Green, gray-green, blue-green; vitreous luster.
Cleavage: Perfect; fracture uneven.
Tenacity: Brittle to nonbrittle.
Crystal Form: Monoclinic; long tabular, acicular, radiating fibrous.
Occurrence: In the oxidation zone.
Associated Minerals: Koettigite, pyrite, symplesite.

4 Halite, California, 1x

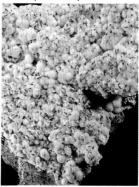

3 Halite, Searles Lake (California), 2x

5 Dundasite, Tasmania (Aust.), 3x

Similar Minerals: Koettigite is indistinguishable from parasymplesite by ordinary methods.

3/4 Halite
(Rock salt)
Hardness: 2.
Density: 2.1–2.2.
Streak: White.
Chemical Formula: NaCl
Color: Colorless, white, reddish, yellow, gray, blue; vitreous luster.
Cleavage: Perfect cubic; fracture conchoidal.
Tenacity: Nonbrittle to brittle.
Crystal Form: Isometric; cubes, massive, granular, fibrous, compact.
Occurrence: In halite deposits, in steppes and deserts, where volcanic gases are vented.
Associated Minerals: Gypsum, anhydrite.
Special Property: Halite is soluble in water.
Similar Minerals: Fluorite is harder and not water soluble.

5 Dundasite
Hardness: 2.
Density: 3.5.
Streak: White.
Chemical Formula:
$Pb_2Al_4(CO_3)_4(OH)_8 \cdot 3H_2O$

Color: White; vitreous to silky luster.
Cleavage: Perfect; fracture uneven.
Tenacity: Brittle.
Crystal Form:
Orthorhombic; acicular, as fibrous crusts.
Occurrence: In the oxidation zone.
Associated Minerals: Crocoite, cerussite.
Similar Minerals: Considering the paragenesisis, dundasite is virtually unmistakable.

145

2 Gypsum, Manitoba (Canada), 1x

If you are careful, you can bend gypsum crystals so that they actually look curved.

1 Gypsum, Hall (Tyrol, Austria), 6x

1/2 Gypsum
Hardness: $1^1/_2$–2.
Density: 2.3–2.4.
Streak: White.
Chemical Formula: $CaSO_4 \cdot 2H_2O$
Color: Colorless, white, yellowish, pink, transparent to opaque; pearly luster.
Cleavage: Perfect; fracture uneven.
Tenacity: Flexible, nonbrittle to brittle.
Crystal Form: Monoclinic; prismatic to tabular, lenticular, acicular, often twinned crystals with reentrant angles (swallowtail twins), fibrous (satin spar, with silky luster),
scaly, granular, compact (alabaster), rosette-shaped ("desert roses").
Occurrence: As crystals and concretionary blocks in clays and marls, in ore deposits, as new formation in old mines, tunnels, and deserts, in salt deposits.
Associated Minerals: Anhydrite, halite, sulfides.
Similar Minerals: Distinguished from all other minerals by its cleavage and hardness.

3 Nacrite
Hardness: 2–$2^1/_2$.
Density: 2.6.
Streak: White.
Chemical Formula: $Al_2Si_2O_5(OH)_4$
Color: White; pearly luster.
Cleavage: Perfect; fracture lamellar.
Tenacity: Nonbrittle.
Crystal Form: Monoclinic; tabular, compact.
Occurrence: In hydrothermal veins, in cavities in volcanic rocks.
Associated Minerals: Quartz, hematite.
Similar Minerals: Kaolinite does not form crystals that

3 Nacrite, Arizona, 3x

4 Phlogopite, Finland, 1x

5 Mellite, Tatabanya (Hungary), 4x

can be seen with the eye, but by ordinary methods it is indistinguishable from compact nacrite.

4 Phlogopite
Hardness: 2–2$^{1}/_{2}$.
Density: 2.75–2.97.
Streak: White.
Chemical Formula: $KMg_3[(F,OH)_2/AlSi_3O_{10}]$
Color: Dark brown, reddish brown, yellowish, greenish; vitreous luster.
Cleavage: Absolutely perfect basal; fracture lamellar.
Tenacity: Thin sheets flexible and elastic.
Crystal Form: Monoclinic; tabular, more rarely prismatic, lamellar, scaly.
Occurrence: In marbles, metamorphic dolomites, and pegmatites.
Associated Minerals: Graphite, calcite, diopside.
Similar Minerals: Biotite appears in a different paragenesis. Diaspore is harder.

5 Mellite
Hardness: 2–2$^{1}/_{2}$.
Density: 1.64.
Streak: White.
Chemical Formula: $C_{12}Al_2O_{12} \cdot 18H_2O$
Color: Brown, black; vitreous to resinous luster.
Cleavage: None; fracture conchoidal.
Tenacity: Only slightly brittle.
Crystal Form: Tetragonal; bipyramidal, massive, lumpy.
Occurrence: In coal deposits.
Associated Minerals: Coal, clay minerals.
Similar Minerals: The low density and the paragenesis of mellite rule out any misidentification.

1 Ettringite, Hotazel (South Africa), 6x

2 Ettringite, Hotazel (S. Africa), 3x

3 Hydrozincite, Iran, 4x

1/2 Ettringite
Hardness: 2–2¹/₂.
Density: 1.77.
Streak: White.
Chemical Formula:
$Ca_6Al_2(SO_4)_3(OH)_{12} \cdot 24H_2O$
Color: Colorless, yellow, white; vitreous luster.
Cleavage: Barely discernible; fracture uneven.
Tenacity: Brittle.
Crystal Form: Hexagonal; prismatic, acicular, fibrous.
Occurrence: In volcanic rocks.
Associated Minerals: Calcite, afwillite, phillipsite.
Similar Minerals: Calcite and afwillite have a different crystal form; calcite has a good cleavage.

3 Hydrozincite
Hardness: 2–2¹/₂.
Density: 3.2–3.8.
Streak: White.
Chemical Formula:
$Zn_5[(OH)_3/CO_3]_2$
Color: White to yellowish, dull.
Cleavage: Usually not discernible because of the development of the mineral; fracture earthy to fibrous.
Tenacity: Nonbrittle.
Crystal Form: Monoclinic; rarely acicular, usually radiated, crusty, earthy.

Occurrence: In the oxidation zone.
Associated Minerals: Smithsonite, hemimorphite, wulfenite.
Special Property: Hydrozincite fluoresces in UV light.
Similar Minerals: The paragenesis makes hydrozincite unmistakable.

4 Pharmacosiderite (containing barium), Clara Mine (Black Forest, Germany), 6x

The Clara Mine near Oberwolfach in the Black Forest is one of the most famous German mineral localities. With over 250 mineral species, it is one of the world's leading localities in terms of the number of species found.

5 Senarmontite, Algeria, 6x

4 Pharmacosiderite

Hardness: $2^{1}/_{2}$.
Density: 2.8–2.9.
Streak: White.
Chemical Formula:
$KFe_4[(OH)_4/(AsO_4)_3] \cdot 7H_2O$
Color: Green, yellow, brown, red; vitreous luster, on fracture surfaces greasy luster.
Cleavage: Barely discernible; fracture conchoidal.
Tenacity: Brittle.
Crystal Form: Isometric; always attached, usually cubes, rarely with octahedron, granular, massive.
Occurrence: In the oxidation zone.

Associated Minerals: Olivenite, clinoclase.
Similar Minerals: Fluorite is harder and is distinguished by its good cleavage.

5 Senarmontite

Hardness: $2–2^{1}/_{2}$.
Density: 5.5.
Streak: White.
Chemical Formula: Sb_2O_3
Color: Colorless, white; vitreous to resinous luster.
Cleavage: None; fracture conchoidal.
Tenacity: Brittle.
Crystal Form: Isometric; octahedral, granular, crusty, massive.

Occurrence: In the oxidation zone.
Associated Minerals: Stibnite, valentinite.
Similar Minerals: The octahedral crystal form and the association with other antimony minerals make any misidentification of senarmontite impossible.

White Streak

1 Muscovite, Brazil, 1x

2 Muscovite, Bavaria (Germany), 2x

3 Schulenbergite, Bad Ems (Germany), 12x

Cryolite once was an important industrial mineral, because it facilitated the recovery of aluminum. Today cryolite is still required for this purpose, but it now is made artificially and recovered again and again.

1/2 Muscovite
Hardness: 2–2¹/₂.
Density: 2.78–2.88.
Streak: White.
Chemical Formula:
$KAl_2[(OH,F)_2/AlSi_3O_{10}]$
Color: Colorless, white, silvery gray, greenish, yellowish, brownish; pearly luster.
Cleavage: Highly perfect basal; fracture lamellar.
Tenacity: Nonbrittle; thin sheets elastic and flexible.
Crystal Form: Monoclinic; tabular, hexagonal, rarely prismatic, lamellar, scaly, rosette-shaped.
Occurrence: In granites, pegmatites, gneisses, mica schists, sandstones, and marbles; not in volcanic rocks.
Associated Minerals: Quartz, feldspar, biotite.
Similar Minerals: Talc and chlorite are softer; biotite and phlogopite are darker.

3 Schulenbergite
Hardness: 2.
Density: 3.4.
Streak: White.
Chemical Formula:
$(Cu,Zn)_7(SO_4,CO_3)_2(OH)$
$\cdot 3H_2O$
Color: Light blue; vitreous to pearly luster.
Cleavage: Perfect; fracture lamellar.
Tenacity: Brittle.
Crystal Form: Trigonal; hexagonal sheets, scaly, globular.
Occurrence: In the oxidation zone.
Associated Minerals: Serpierite, linarite.
Similar Minerals: Devillite is indistinguishable from schulenbergite by ordinary methods.

4 Cryolite, Greenland, 1x

5 Wulfenite, Carinthia (Austria), 2x   6 Wulfenite, Los Lamentos (Mexico), 4x

4 Cryolite

Hardness: 2¹/₂–3.
Density: 2.95.
Streak: White.
Chemical Formula: Na_3AlF_6
Color: Colorless, white, yellowish, black, violet; vitreous luster.
Cleavage: Often visible; fracture uneven.
Tenacity: Brittle.
Crystal Form: Monoclinic; pseudocubic crystals, but usually massive.
Occurrence: In pegmatites.
Associated Minerals: Siderite, fluorite, topaz, quartz.
Similar Minerals: Fluorite has a different cleavage and is harder. Topaz is harder.

5 Wulfenite

Hardness: 3.
Density: 6.7–6.9.
Streak: White.
Chemical Formula: $PbMoO_4$
Color: Yellow to orange-red, blue, gray; adamantine to resinous luster.
Cleavage: Poor pyramidal; fracture conchoidal.
Tenacity: Brittle.
Crystal Form: Tetragonal; steep pyramids, thick to thin tabular, acicular, massive.
Occurrence: In the oxidation zone.
Associated Minerals: Galena, cerussite, hydrozincite, pyromorphite, smithsonite.
Similar Minerals: The appearance and the association of wulfenite with other lead and zinc oxidation minerals rule out any misidentification.

151

1 Vanadinite, Arizona, 6x

2 Vanadinite, Arizona, 3x

3 Hydroboracite, Harz Mountains (Germany), 0.5x

1/2 Vanadinite
Hardness: 3.
Density: 6.8–7.1.
Streak: White, yellowish.
Chemical Formula:
$Pb_5[Cl/(VO_4)_3]$
Color: Yellow, brown, orange, red; adamantine to greasy luster.
Cleavage: None; fracture conchoidal.
Tenacity: Brittle.
Crystal Form: Hexagonal; prismatic to tabular, radiating fibrous, globular, massive.
Occurrence: In the oxidation zone.
Associated Minerals: Wulfenite, calcite, descloizite.
Similar Minerals: Apatite is harder. Pyromorphite and mimetite are not red.

3 Hydroboracite
Hardness: 2–3.
Density: 2.2.
Streak: White.
Chemical Formula:
$CaMgB_6O_{11} \cdot 6H_2O$
Color: White, brownish; vitreous luster.
Cleavage: Perfect; fracture uneven.
Tenacity: Brittle.
Crystal Form: Monoclinic; acicular, radiating fibrous, fine granular, massive.
Occurrence: In salt deposits.
Associated Minerals: Halite, anhydrite.
Similar Minerals: The paragenesis makes acicular hydroboracite unmistakable.

4 Valentinite
Hardness: 2–3.
Density: 5.6–5.8.
Streak: White.
Chemical Formula:
Sb_2O_3
Color: Colorless, white, yellowish, gray; adamantine to pearly luster.
Cleavage: Perfect; fracture uneven.
Tenacity: Nonbrittle.

4 Valentinite, Czechoslovakia, 2x

5 Phosgenite, Lavrion (Greece), 4x

6 Duftite, Tsumeb (Namibia), 8x

Crystal Form:
Orthorhombic; prismatic to acicular, radiated, granular, massive.
Occurrence: In the oxidation zone.
Associated Minerals: Stibnite, senarmontite.
Similar Minerals: The high luster and the acicular development make valentinite unmistakable.

5 Phosgenite
Hardness: $2^1/_2$–3.

Density: 6.0–6.3.
Streak: White.
Chemical Formula:
$Pb_2[Cl_2/CO_3]$

Color: Colorless, white, gray, brown, yellow; greasy to adamantine luster.
Cleavage: Perfect; fracture conchoidal.
Tenacity: Nonbrittle.
Crystal Form: Tetragonal; short columnar, tabular, long prismatic, acicular.
Occurrence: In the oxidation zone.
Associated Minerals: Cerussite, anglesite.
Similar Minerals: Cerussite and anglesite have a different crystal form.

6 Duftite
Hardness: 3.
Density: 6.4.
Streak: Whitish.
Chemical Formula:
$CuPbAsO_4OH$
Color: green; vitreous luster.
Cleavage: Not discernible; fracture uneven.
Tenacity: Brittle.
Crystal Form:
Orthorhombic; thick tabular, crusty.
Occurrence: In the oxidation zone.
Associated Minerals: Cerussite, azurite.
Similar Minerals: Olivenite has a different crystal form.

1 Anglesite, Siegerland (Germany), 8x

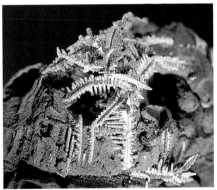
3 Silver, Hartenstein (Germany), 1x

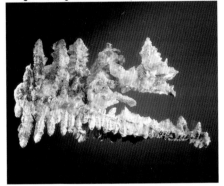
2 Silver, Wittichen (Germany), 2x

4 Silver, Aue (Saxony, Germany), 3x

1 Anglesite
Hardness: 3.
Density: 6.3.
Streak: White.
Chemical Formula: $PbSO_4$
Color: Colorless, white, yellowish, brownish, gray.
Cleavage: Visible basal; fracture conchoidal.
Tenacity: Brittle.
Crystal Form: Orthorhombic; tabular, prismatic, bipyramidal, acicular, granular, crusty, massive.
Occurrence: In the oxidation zone.
Associated Minerals: Cerussite, galena, phosgenite.
Similar Minerals: Barite has a better cleavage. Cerussite, in contrast to anglesite, often has twins and trillings.

2/3/4 Silver
Hardness: 2¹/₂–3.
Density: 9.6–12.
Streak: Silver-white, metallic.
Chemical Formula: Ag
Color: Silver-white, often with yellowish to blackish tarnish.
Cleavage: None; fracture hackly.
Tenacity: Nonbrittle, very ductile, can be hammered into thin plates.
Crystal Form: Isometric; predominantly cubes, dendritic, in sheets and wire shapes, massive.
Occurrence: In hydrothermal veins.
Associated Minerals: Argentite, pyrargyrite, proustite, galena.
Similar Minerals: Galena and other silver-gray minerals, with the exception of argentite, cannot be hammered into thin plates. Argentite has a dark streak.

5 Biotite, Eifel (Germany), 2x

The lithium mica lepidolite can be an important ore of lithium. Although it does not at all resemble an ore mineral (it is pink to silvery and not especially heavy), miners call it an ore because of its high content of lithium, an alkali metal.

6 Lepidolite, Himalaya Mine (California), 4x

5 Biotite

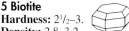

Hardness: $2^1/_2$–3.
Density: 2.8–3.2.
Streak: White.
Chemical Formula:
$K(Mg,Fe)_3[(OH)_2/(Al,Fe)Si_3O_{10}]$
Color: Dark brown, dark green, black, reddish; pearly luster.
Cleavage: Highly perfect; fracture lamellar.
Tenacity: Nonbrittle; thin sheets flexible and elastic.
Crystal Form: Monoclinic; tabular, hexagonal, rosette-shaped, rarely prismatic, thin sheets, scales.
Occurrence: In granites, pegmatites, gneisses, mica schists, diorites, hornfels, volcanic rocks.
Associated Minerals: Quartz, muscovite, feldspar.
Similar Minerals: Chlorite and talc are softer. Muscovite is a different color.

6 Lepidolite

Hardness: 2–$2^1/_2$.
Density: 2.8–2.9.
Streak: White.
Chemical Formula:
$KLi_2Al[(F,OH)_2/Si_4O_{10}]$
Color: Pink, lilac, reddish; vitreous to pearly luster.
Cleavage: Highly perfect basal; fracture lamellar.
Tenacity: Nonbrittle; thin sheets flexible and elastic.
Crystal Form: Monoclinic; tabular, prismatic, lamellar, scaly, compact.
Occurrence: In pegmatites, in pneumatolytic veins.
Associated Minerals: Tourmaline, feldspar, quartz.
Similar Minerals: Muscovite, when it contains manganese (alurgite), may also be pink to reddish.

155

1 Koettigite, Mapimi (Mexico), 6x

2 Gibbsite, Lavrion (Greece), 2x

The zinc arsenate koettigite is closely related to the nickel arsenate annabergite and the cobalt arsenate erythrite. For this reason it has the same crystal forms they do.

1 Koettigite
Hardness: 2¹/₂–3.
Density: 3.3.
Streak: White.
Chemical Formula:
$Zn_3(AsO_4)_2 \cdot 8H_2O$
Color: White, gray, brown, reddish; vitreous luster.
Cleavage: Perfect; fracture uneven.
Tenacity: Slightly flexible.
Crystal Form: Monoclinic; prismatic, long tabular, radiating fibrous, massive.
Occurrence: In the oxidation zone.
Associated Minerals: Adamite.
Similar Minerals: Unmistakable.

2 Gibbsite
Hardness: 2¹/₂–3¹/₂.
Density: 2.4.
Streak: White.
Chemical Formula:
$Al(OH)_3$
Color: White, light blue, greenish, gray; vitreous luster.
Cleavage: Usually not discernible; fracture uneven.
Tenacity: Brittle.
Crystal Form: Monoclinic; tabular, massive, reniform, crusty.
Occurrence: In the oxidation zone.
Associated Minerals: Azurite, hydrozincite, aurichalcite.

Similar Minerals: Glaucokerinite is distinctly softer.

3 Zinnwaldite
Hardness: 2¹/₂–3.
Density: 2.9–3.3.
Streak: White.
Chemical Formula:
$K(Li,Al,Fe)_3(Al,Si)_4O_{10}(OH,F)_2$
Color: Silver-gray to greenish; vitreous luster.
Cleavage: Perfect; fracture lamellar.
Tenacity: Flexible.
Crystal Form: Monoclinic; tabular, lamellar.
Occurrence: In pegmatites

3 Zinnwaldite, Cornwall (Eng.), 2x

4 Astrophyllite, Kola Peninsula (Russia), 3x

Weinschenkite was named for the famous Bavarian mineralogist Weinschenk. In the English-speaking world the name churchite is better known.

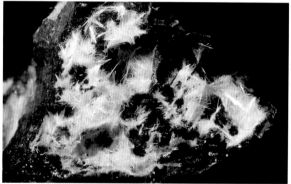

5 Churchite, Auerbach (Bavaria, Germany), 4x

and tin deposits.
Associated Minerals: Topaz, cassiterite, feldspar, fluorite.
Similar Minerals: Muscovite is indistinguishable by ordinary methods. Biotite and phlogopite are more brown or black, lepidolite more pink.

4 Astrophyllite
Hardness: 3.
Density: 3.3–3.4.
Streak: White.
Chemical Formula: $(K,Na)_3(Fe,Mn)_7Ti_2[(O,OH)_7/Si_8O_{24}]$
Color: Yellowish, greenish olive; metallic vitreous luster.

Cleavage: Perfect; fracture lamellar.
Tenacity: Brittle.
Crystal Form: Triclinic; tabular, lamellar, often intergrown in radiated groups.
Occurrence: In alkali rocks, pegmatites.
Associated Minerals: Quartz, feldspar, aegirine.
Similar Minerals: The mica minerals are not brittle.

5 Churchite
(Weinschenkite)
Hardness: 3.
Density: 3.3.
Streak: White.

Chemical Formula: $(Y,Er)PO_4 \cdot H_2O$
Color: White; vitreous to silky luster.
Cleavage: Not discernible; fracture fibrous.
Tenacity: Brittle.
Crystal Form: Monoclinic; acicular, fibrous.
Occurrence: In phosphate deposits.
Associated Minerals: Limonite, cacoxenite, beraunite.
Similar Minerals: Wavellite almost never has fibers as fine as those of churchite; it usually displays only pinacoid faces.

1 Strunzite, Hagendorf (Bavaria, Germany), 4x

3 Calcite twin, Ulm (Germany), 2x

2 Calcite, Siegerland (Germany), 2x

4 Calcite, Harz Mountains (Germany), 2x

1 Strunzite
Hardness: 3.
Density: 2.52.
Streak: White.
Chemical Formula:
$MnFe_2[OH/PO_4]_2$
Color: Straw-yellow;
vitreous luster.
Cleavage: None; fracture
uneven.
Tenacity: Brittle.
Crystal Form: Triclinic;
acicular to capillary, very
rarely prismatic.
Occurrence: In phosphate
pegmatites, in limonite
deposits.
Associated Minerals:
Beraunite, rockbridgeite,
laueite.
Similar Minerals: Cacoxene
is more golden yellow, but is
often indistinguishable from
strunzite by ordinary methods.

2/3/4/5/6 Calcite
Hardness: 3.
Density: 2.6–2.8.
Streak: White.
Chemical Formula: $CaCO_3$
Color: Colorless, white, yel-
low, brown; variously tinted
by inclusions; vitreous luster.
Cleavage: Highly perfect
along basic rhombohedral
planes; fracture sparry to
conchoidal.
Tenacity: Brittle.

Crystal Form: Trigonal.
Scalenohedrons, rhombo-
hedrons, or prisms with base;
habit prismatic, lenticular,
acicular, thick and thin
tabular; often also radiated,
globular, reniform, in the
form of dripstones, massive.
Occurrence: In druses of ore
veins, vesicles in volcanic
rocks, lining fissures and in

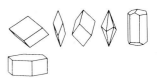

6 Calcite, Harz Mountains (Germany), 3x

5 Calcite, Serifos (Greece), 3x

7 Pachnolite, Greenland, 4x

druses of carbonate rocks, as a gangue mineral in many hydrothermal veins; rock-forming, igneous in carbonatites, sedimentary in limestones, metamorphic in marbles.
Associated Minerals: Dolomite, quartz, ore minerals, and many others.
Special Property: Calcite effervesces with cold dilute hydrochloric acid.
Similar Minerals: Dolomite,

in contrast to calcite, effervesces only with hot hydrochloric acid. Quartz is harder. Gypsum is softer. Anhydrite does not effervesce with hydrochloric acid.

7 Pachnolite

Hardness: 3.
Density: 2.98.
Streak: White.
Chemical Formula: $CaNaAlF_6 \cdot H_2O$
Color: Colorless, white, brownish if limonite is present; vitreous luster.
Cleavage: Barely discernible; fracture conchoidal.

Tenacity: Brittle.
Crystal Form: Monoclinic; prismatic, with steep pyramidal pinacoid faces, rarely tabular.
Occurrence: Lining druses in pegmatites.
Associated Minerals: Thomsenolite, ralstonite, cryolite.
Similar Minerals: Thomsenolite has a better cleavage and usually displays distinctly monoclinic crystals, slanting on one side.

159

1 Laueite, Hagendorf (Bavaria, Germany), 10x

2 Paralaurionite, Lavrion (Greece), 10x

3 Klebelsbergite, Tuscany (Italy), 6x

Paralaurionite and numerous other minerals from Lavrion (Greece) come from very old slags that were thrown into the sea by the ancient Greeks. There, in cavities in the slags, new minerals were able to form from lead residue and the chlorine in the sea water.

1 Laueite
Hardness: 3.
Density: 2.49.
Streak: White to yellowish.
Chemical Formula:
$MnFe_2[OH/PO_4] \cdot 8H_2O$
Color: Yellow, orange-yellow, honey-brown; vitreous luster.
Cleavage: Not very visible; fracture conchoidal.
Tenacity: Brittle.
Crystal Form: Triclinic; prismatic; thick tabular, in crusts.
Occurrence: In phosphate pegmatites.
Associated Minerals: Strunzite, stewartite.

Similar Minerals: Stewartite has a different crystal form and is much more thin tabular.

2 Paralaurionite
Hardness: 3.
Density: 6.2.
Streak: White.
Chemical Formula:
PbClOH
Color: Colorless, white, yellow; vitreous to adamantine luster.
Cleavage: Perfect; fracture fibrous.
Tenacity: Nonbrittle, flexible but inelastic.
Crystal Form: Monoclinic; long tabular, prismatic, thin tabular, acicular.
Occurrence: In the oxidation zone and ancient lead slags.
Associated Minerals: Phosgenite, laurionite, fiedlerite.
Similar Minerals: Laurionite is brittle. Fiedlerite has a different crystal form.

3 Klebelsbergite
Hardness: 3.
Density: 3.5.
Streak: White.
Chemical Formula:
$Sb_4O_4(OH)_2 \cdot SO_4$
Color: White to yellow; vitreous luster.

4 Vauxite, Bolivia, 1x

5 Paravauxite, Bolivia, 4x

6 Paravauxite, Lallagua (Bolivia), 6x

Cleavage: Not discernible; fracture uneven.
Tenacity: Brittle.
Crystal Form: Orthorhombic; acicular, long tabular, often vertically striated, radiating fibrous.
Occurrence: In the oxidation zone.
Associated Minerals: Antimonite, valentinite.
Similar Minerals: Considering the paragenesis with stibnite, klebelsbergite is unmistakable.

4 Vauxite
Hardness: 3½.
Density: 2.4.

Streak: White.
Chemical Formula: $FeAl_2(PO_4)_2(OH)_2 \cdot 6H_2O$
Color: Blue; vitreous luster.
Cleavage: None; fracture conchoidal.
Tenacity: Brittle.
Crystal Form: Triclinic; tabular, radiating fibrous, globular.
Occurrence: In the oxidation zone.
Associated Minerals: Paravauxite, wavellite, cassiterite.
Similar Minerals: The color and characteristic paragenesis of vauxite make any misidentification impossible.

5/6 Paravauxite
Hardness: 3.
Density: 2.38.
Streak: White.
Chemical Formula: $FeAl_2(PO_4)_2(OH)_2 \cdot 8H_2O$
Color: Colorless to greenish white; vitreous luster.
Cleavage: Perfect; fracture conchoidal.
Tenacity: Brittle.
Crystal Form: Triclinic; tabular, radiating fibrous.
Occurrence: In the oxidation zone.
Associated Minerals: Wavellite, quartz.
Similar Minerals: Laueite is a different color.

161

1 Barite, Dreislar (Sauerland, Germany), 0.5x

2 Barite, Morocco, 1x

3 Scholzite, Hagendorf (Ger.), 6x

1/2 Barite
Hardness: 3–3$\frac{1}{2}$.
Density: 4.48.
Streak: White.
Chemical Formula: $BaSO_4$
Color: Colorless, white, yellowish, reddish, blue; pearly luster.
Cleavage: Perfect basal; fracture sparry to conchoidal.
Tenacity: Brittle.
Crystal Form:
Orthorhombic; tabular, more rarely prismatic; fan-shaped, cockscomb-shaped, in sands also flower-shaped ("barite roses" or "crested barite"), sparry, often massive.
Occurrence: As gangue mineral in hydrothermal veins, where beautiful crystals often occur in druses; as concretions in sandstones and other sedimentary rocks.
Associated Minerals:
Calcite, quartz, fluorite, ore minerals.
Similar Minerals: Quartz and feldspar are harder. Gypsum, calcite, aragonite are much lighter. Massive celestite often is indistinguishable from barite by ordinary methods.

3 Scholzite
Hardness: 3–4.
Density: 3.11.
Streak: White.
Chemical Formula:
$CaZn_2[PO_4] \cdot 2H_2O$
Color: Colorless, white, yellowish; vitreous luster.
Cleavage: Barely visible; fracture conchoidal.
Tenacity: Brittle.
Crystal Form:
Orthorhombic; tabular to acicular, radiated.
Occurrence: In phosphate pegmatites.
Associated Minerals:
Phosphophyllite, hopeite, parahopeite, tarbuttite.

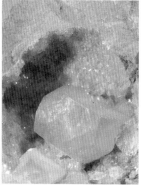

4 Celestite, Rüdersdorf (Ger.), 1x

5 Celestite, Poland, 2x

6 Weloganite, Montreal (Canada), 10x

Similar Minerals:
Considering the paragenesis, unmistakable.

4/5 Celestite
(Celestine)
Hardness: 3–3$\frac{1}{2}$.
Density: 3.9–4.0.
Streak: White.
Chemical Formula: $SrSO_4$
Color: Colorless, white, blue, reddish, greenish, brownish; vitreous luster, on cleavage surfaces pearly luster.
Cleavage: Perfect basal, two additional cleavage directions are much poorer; fracture uneven.
Tenacity: Brittle.

Crystal Form:
Orthorhombic; thin to thick tabular, prismatic, radiating fibrous, bladed, fibrous, granular, earthy.
Occurrence: In hydrothermal veins and vesicles in volcanic rocks, in limestones and marls.
Associated Minerals:
Calcite, pyrite, barite.
Similar Minerals: Barite has a greater density. Calcite effervesces with hydrochloric acid. Gypsum is much softer.

6 Weloganite
Hardness: 4.
Density: 3.2.
Streak: White.
Chemical Formula:
$Sr_5ZrC_9H_8O_{31}$
Color: White, yellowish; vitreous luster.
Cleavage: Perfect; fracture conchoidal.
Crystal Form: Hexagonal; crystals tapering at one end.
Occurrence: In alkali rocks.
Associated Minerals:
Strontianite, dawsonite.
Similar Minerals:
Unmistakable.

163

2 Cerussite, Siegerland (Germany), 6x

3 Cerussite, Siegerland (Germany), 4x

1 Cerussite, Arizona, 6x

1/2/3 Cerussite
Hardness: 3–3$^{1}/_{2}$.
Density: 6.4–6.6.
Streak: White.
Chemical Formula: $PbCO_3$
Color: Colorless, white, gray, yellow, brown, blackish (from inclusions of galena); greasy to adamantine luster.
Cleavage: Not easily discernible; fracture conchoidal.
Tenacity: Brittle.
Crystal Form: Orthorhombic; prismatic, isometric, tabular, reniform, crusty, earthy; often geniculated twins; multiple twinning creates star-shaped and honeycomb-shaped structures.
Occurrence: In the oxidation zone.
Associated Minerals: Galena, pyromorphite, smithsonite, anglesite.
Similar Minerals: Calcite and anhydrite effervesce with dilute hydrochloric acid. The characteristic twinning distinguishes cerussite from anglesite.

4 Ferrierite
Hardness: 3–3$^{1}/_{2}$.
Density: 2.1.
Streak: White.
Chemical Formula: $(Na,K)_2MgAl_3Si_{15}O_{36}OH \cdot 9H_2O$
Color: White, reddish; vitreous luster.
Cleavage: Not discernible; fracture uneven.
Tenacity: Brittle.
Crystal Form: Orthorhombic; acicular, radiating fibrous.
Occurrence: In cavities in volcanic rocks.
Associated Minerals: Calcite, heulandite.

4 Ferrierite, Sardinia (Italy), 4x

5 Laurionite, Lavrion (Greece), 8x

6 Anhydrite, Tuscany (Italy), 6x

Similar Minerals: Ferrierite is indistinguishable from natrolite and scolecite by ordinary methods.

5 Laurionite
Hardness: 3–3½.
Density: 6.10–6.24.
Streak: White.
Chemical Formula: PbOHCl
Color: Colorless to white; vitreous to adamantine luster.
Cleavage: Barely discernible; fracture uneven.
Tenacity: Brittle.
Crystal Form: Orthorhombic; long tabular to acicular, with typical V-shaped striation.
Occurrence: In cavities in antique lead slags.
Associated Minerals: Fiedlerite, paralaurionite, cerussite.
Similar Minerals: Paralaurionite is nonbrittle.

6 Anhydrite
Hardness: 3–3½.
Density: 2.98.
Streak: White.
Chemical Formula: $CaSO_4$
Color: Colorless, white, gray, blue; vitreous luster.
Cleavage: Perfect; cleavage products ashlar-shaped, with right angles. Fracture sparry.
Tenacity: Brittle.
Crystal Form: Orthorhombic; tabular, prismatic, granular, sparry, massive.
Occurrence: In salt deposits, sediments, hydrothermal veins.
Associated Minerals: Gypsum, halite.
Similar Minerals: The characteristic cleavage at right angles makes anhydrite easy to recognize. Calcite effervesces with dilute hydrochloric acid.

165

1 Adamite, Mapimi (Mexico), 6x

3 Cuproadamite, Tsumeb (Namibia), 2x

2 Adamite, Mapimi (Mexico), 8x

4 Strontianite, Dreislar (Germany), 3x

1/2/3 Adamite

Hardness: $3½$.
Density: 4.3–4.5.
Streak: White.
Chemical Formula:
$Zn_2[OH/AsO_4]$
Color: Colorless, white, yellow, green (contains copper = copper adamite), pink to violet (contains cobalt = cobalt adamite); vitreous luster.
Cleavage: Perfect; fracture conchoidal.
Tenacity: Brittle.
Crystal Form: Orthorhombic; prismatic to acicular, radiating fibrous, massive.
Occurrence: In the oxidation zone.
Associated Minerals: Smithsonite, azurite, hemimorphite, aurichalcite.
Similar Minerals: Olivenite is always darker green, but sometimes cannot be distinguished from copper adamite by ordinary methods.

4 Strontianite

Hardness: $3½$.
Density: 3.7.
Streak: White.
Chemical Formula: $SrCO_3$
Color: Colorless, white, yellowish, greenish, gray; vitreous luster, on fracture surfaces greasy luster.
Cleavage: Discernible; fracture conchoidal.
Tenacity: Brittle.
Crystal Form: Orthorhombic; acicular, spear-shaped, often intergrown in tufts, sometimes curved, rarely prismatic or bipyramidal, radiating fibrous, massive.
Occurrence: In hydrothermal veins, as cavity filling in chalks.
Associated Minerals: Calcite, ore minerals.
Similar Minerals: Calcite and aragonite effervesce readily with cold dilute hydrochloric acid.

White Streak

5 Fiedlerite, Lavrion (Greece), 8x

Fiedlerite was named for the Saxon mining official Fiedler, who in the nineteenth century explored the Greek ore deposits for the king of Greece.

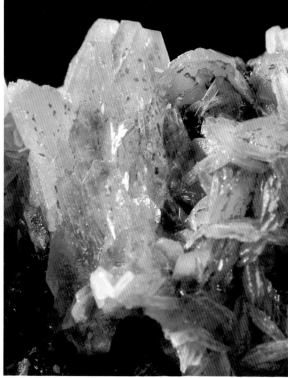

6 Ludlamite, La Union (Spain), 8x

5 Fiedlerite
Hardness: $3^1/_2$.
Density: 5.8.
Streak: White.
Chemical Formula:
$Pb_3Cl_4(OH)_2$
Color: Colorless, white; adamantine luster.
Cleavage: Not easily discernible; fracture conchoidal.
Tenacity: Brittle.
Crystal Form: Monoclinic; tabular, only in crystals.
Occurrence: In ancient lead slags.
Associated Minerals: Paralaurionite, laurionite, phosgenite.
Similar Minerals: There is no possibility of misidentification, considering the occurrence of fiedlerite and its characteristic crystal form.

6 Ludlamite
Hardness: 3–4.
Density: 3.1.
Streak: White.
Chemical Formula:
$Fe_3[PO_4]_2 \cdot 4H_2O$
Color: Light green to green; vitreous luster.
Cleavage: Perfect basal; fracture uneven.
Tenacity: Brittle.
Crystal Form: Monoclinic; pseudo-octahedral, tabular, as massive, sparry aggregates.
Occurrence: In phosphate pegmatites, as lining in hydrothermal ore deposits.
Associated Minerals: Vivianite, pyrite.
Similar Minerals: Ludlamite's color and cleavage make misidentification impossible.

167

1 Siderite, Neudorf (Harz Mountains, Germany), 2x

3 Siderite, Siegerland (Germany), 2x

2 Siderite, Neudorf (Harz Mountains, Germany), 2x

4 Paradamite, Mexico, 6x

1/2/3 Siderite
Hardness: 4–4¹/₂.
Density: 3.7–3.9.
Streak: White.
Chemical Formula: $FeCO_3$
Color: Yellowish white, yellowish brown to dark brown, sometimes with bluish tarnish; vitreous luster.
Cleavage: Perfect rhombohedral; fracture sparry.
Tenacity: Brittle.
Crystal Form: Trigonal. Rhombohedral, often curved into saddle shapes; rarely scalenohedral, often massive.
Occurrence: In pegmatites in hydrothermal veins, in metasomatically altered chalks, as concretions in peat moors.
Associated Minerals: Chalcedony, barite, calcite, ore minerals.
Similar Minerals: Calcite effervesces readily with dilute hydrochloric acid. Sphalerite has a different cleavage.

4 Paradamite
Hardness: 3¹/₂.
Density: 4.55.
Streak: White.
Chemical Formula: Zn_2AsO_4OH
Color: Yellowish; vitreous luster.
Cleavage: Perfect; fracture uneven.
Crystal Form: Triclinic; tabular, often rounded.
Occurrence: In the oxidation zone.
Associated Minerals: Limonite, adamite, mimetite.
Similar Minerals: Adamite has a different crystal form.

5 Serpierite
Hardness: 3¹/₂–4.
Density: 3.08.
Streak: White.
Chemical Formula: $Ca(Cu,Zn)_4[(OH)_6/(SO_4)_2] \cdot 3H_2O$
Color: Blue; vitreous luster.

5 Serpierite, Bad Ems (Ger.), 10x

Aragonite has the same chemical composition as calcite, which is far more common, but it is distinguished from calcite by its crystal structure and crystal form.

6 Aragonite, Harz Mountains (Germany), 2x

Cleavage: Perfect; fracture uneven.
Tenacity: Brittle.
Crystal Form: Monoclinic; acicular, radiated.
Occurrence: In the oxidation zone.
Associated Minerals: Gypsum, spangolite, devillite.
Similar Minerals: Unlike serpierite, linarite turns white with hydrochloric acid. Devillite is more lamellar and/or foamy.

6 Aragonite
Hardness: $3^{1}/_{2}$–4.
Density: 2.95.
Streak: White.
Chemical Formula: $CaCO_3$
Color: Colorless, white, gray, red to reddish violet; vitreous luster.
Cleavage: Indistinct; fracture conchoidal.
Tenacity: Brittle.
Crystal Form: Orthorhombic; usually acicular, prismatic, spatulate, trillings resemble hexagonal prisms; radiated, granular, wormlike structures known as *flos ferri*, "flowers of iron."
Occurrence: In the oxidation zone, in druses and lining cavities in effusive rocks, embedded in clays (here, usually trillings), in the deposits of hot springs.
Associated Minerals: Zeolites, quartz, oxidation minerals.
Special Property: Effervesces with dilute hydrochloric acid.
Similar Minerals: Calcite is distinguished from aragonite by its cleavage; all other minerals are distinguishable by the hydrochloric acid test.

1 Laumontite, Ticino (Switzerland), 6x

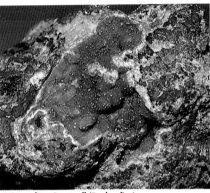

3 Scorodite, Cornwall (England), 4x

2 Scorodite, Black Forest (Germany), 4x

Laumontite belongs to the zeolite family—a group of minerals that give off water when heated, while their crystal structure is left intact.

1 Laumontite
Hardness: 3¹/₂.
Density: 2.25–2.35.
Streak: White.
Chemical Formula:
$Ca[Al_2Si_4O_{12}] \cdot 4H_2O$
Color: Colorless, white (with water loss); vitreous luster, on cleavage surfaces pearly luster.
Cleavage: Perfect in the longitudinal direction of the crystals; fracture uneven.
Tenacity: Brittle.
Crystal Form: Monoclinic; prisms with typically slanted pinacoid faces; radiated, massive.
Occurrence: In druses of pegmatites, granites, in vesicles in volcanic rocks.
Associated Minerals: Apophyllite, stilbite, chabazite.
Similar Minerals: The crystal form of laumontite crystals makes any misidentification impossible.

2/3 Scorodite
Hardness: 3¹/₂–4.
Density: 3.1–3.3.
Streak: White.
Chemical Formula:
$Fe[AsO_4] \cdot 2H_2O$
Color: Colorless, white, yellow, greenish, blue, brown; greasy vitreous luster.
Cleavage: Barely discernible; fracture conchoidal.
Tenacity: Brittle.
Crystal Form:
Orthorhombic; tabular to bipyramidal, radiating fibrous, crusty, as coating.
Occurrence: In the oxidation zone.
Associated Minerals: Arseniosiderite, olivenite, adamite.
Similar Minerals:
Considering the crystal form and paragenesis with other arsenic-containing minerals, misidentification is out of the question.

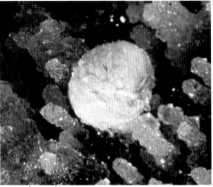

4 Gyrolite, India, 4x

6 Wavellite, Arkansas, 2x

5 Wavellite, Arkansas, 4x

7 Wavellite, England, 1x

4 Gyrolite
Hardness: 3¹/₂–4.
Density: 3–4.
Streak: White.
Chemical Formula:
$Ca_2Si_3O_7(OH)_2 \cdot H_2O$
Color: Colorless, white, greenish, brown, black; vitreous luster.
Cleavage: Perfect; fracture uneven.
Tenacity: Brittle.
Crystal Form: Hexagonal; globular, extremely lamellar.
Occurrence: In cavities in volcanic rocks.
Associated Minerals: Prehnite, apophyllite.
Similar Minerals: Prehnite always forms much thicker tabular crystals.

5/6/7 Wavellite
Hardness: 4.
Density: 2.3–2.4.
Streak: White.
Chemical Formula:
$Al_3[(OH)_3/(PO_4)_2] \cdot 5H_2O$
Color: Colorless, white, yellow, green; vitreous luster.
Cleavage: Not visible; fracture uneven.
Tenacity: Brittle.
Crystal Form: Monoclinic; acicular, radiated, as globular aggregates.
Occurrence: Lining cavities in chert, decomposed granite, limestone.
Associated Minerals: Strengite, cacoxenite.
Similar Minerals: Natrolite and prehnite are harder. Calcite and aragonite effervesce with hydrochloric acid.

171

White Streak

1 Nadorite, Algeria, 4x

3 Stilbite, Hollersbachtal (Austria), 2x

2 Stilbite, Harz Mountains (Germany), 2x

Typical of stilbite are the sheaflike or bonelike aggregates. They are created when many single individuals are closely intergrown, with only tiny angles separating each one from its neighbor.

1 Nadorite
Hardness: 3–4.
Density: 7.02.
Streak: White.
Chemical Formula: PbSbO$_2$Cl
Color: White, yellow, brown; resinous luster.
Cleavage: Perfect; fracture conchoidal.
Tenacity: Brittle.
Crystal Form: Orthorhombic; thin tabular, lenticular, globular.
Occurrence: In antimony deposits.
Associated Minerals: Stibiconite, valentinite.
Similar Minerals: Considering the paragenesis, nadorite is unmistakable.

2/3 Stilbite
Hardness: 3½–4.
Density: 2.1–2.2.
Streak: White.
Chemical Formula: Ca[Al$_2$Si7O$_{18}$] · 7H$_2$O
Color: Colorless, yellow, white, brown; vitreous luster, on cleavage surfaces pearly luster.
Cleavage: Perfect; fracture uneven.
Tenacity: Brittle.
Crystal Form: Monoclinic; prismatic, often intergrown to form sheaflike tufts, globular, radiating fibrous.
Occurrence: In volcanic rocks, druses and cavities in pegmatites, granites, and other igneous rocks, in ore veins.
Associated Minerals: Heulandite, chabazite, scolecite, calcite, laumontite.
Similar Minerals: The typical crystal form of stilbite makes misidentification almost impossible.

4 Strengite, Pleystein (Germany), 2x

6 Strengite, Svappavaara (Sweden), 4x

5 Serpentine, Ireland, 1x

4/6 Strengite

Hardness: 3–4.
Density: 2.87.
Streak: White.
Chemical Formula:
$Fe[PO_4] \cdot 2H_2O$
Color: Colorless, white, yellow, pink, violet; vitreous luster.
Cleavage: Perfect basal; fracture conchoidal.
Tenacity: Brittle.
Crystal Form:
Orthorhombic; tabular, radiating fibrous, as crusts, coatings.
Occurrence: In phosphorus-containing limonite deposits and phosphate pegmatites.
Associated Minerals:
Phosphosiderite, strunzite, beraunite.
Similar Minerals:
Phosphosiderite has a different crystal form, but in radiating fibrous aggregates it is not easily distinguishable from strengite.

5 Serpentine
Hardness: 3–4.
Density: 2.5–2.6.
Streak: White.
Chemical Formula:
$Mg_6[(OH)_8/Si_4O_{10}]$
Color: White, all shades of green, yellow; greasy to silky luster.
Cleavage: Usually not discernible because of the development; fracture conchoidal to fibrous.
Tenacity: Nonbrittle.
Crystal Form: Monoclinic; antigorite in lamellar shapes, usually fine-grained, compact; chrysotile (asbestos) fibrous, capillary.
Occurrence: Rock-forming in serpentinites, with chrysotile lining fissures in them.
Associated Minerals:
Olivine, talc, magnetite, dolomite.
Similar Minerals: Talc is softer. Hornblende asbestos is brittle.

1 Pyromorphite, Bad Ems (Germany), 0.5x

3 Pyromorphite, Black Forest (Germany), 3x

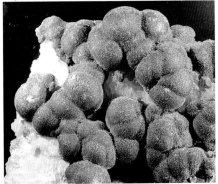
2 Pyromorphite, Siegerland (Germany), 1x

4 Pyromorphite, Siegerland (Germany), 4x

1/2/3/4 Pyromorphite

Hardness: 3½–4.
Density: 6.7–7.0.
Streak: White.
Chemical Formula:
$Pb_5[Cl/(PO_4)_3]$
Color: Green, brown, orange, white, colorless; greasy luster.
Cleavage: None; fracture conchoidal.
Tenacity: Brittle.
Crystal Form: Hexagonal; prismatic crystals, often in barrel-shaped forms due to bent prism faces, acicular, radiating fibrous, crusty, reniform, earthy.
Occurrence: In the oxidation zone of extremely diverse types of lead deposits, particularly in their upper portions, exposed to weathering; the phosphorus needed for formation is often of plant and animal origin.
Associated Minerals: Galena, cerussite, wulfenite, hemimorphite.
Similar Minerals: Mimetite often is hard to distinguish from pyromorphite by ordinary methods, but association with arsenic-containing minerals can provide a clue.

5 Mimetite, Johanngeorgensstadt (Saxony, Germany), 6x

Pyromorphite commonly forms barrel-shaped, domed prisms. Because this development is characteristic of the Bad Ems mining region, such crystals are popularly known as "Emser barrels."

6 Mimetite, Tsumeb (Namibia), 6x

5/6 Mimetite

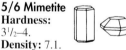

Hardness: $3^{1}/_{2}$–4.
Density: 7.1.
Streak: White.
Chemical Formula: $Pb_5Cl(AsO_4)_3$
Color: Colorless, white, brown, orange, yellow, green, gray; adamantine to greasy luster.
Cleavage: None; fracture conchoidal.
Tenacity: Brittle.
Crystal Form: Hexagonal. Crystals prismatic, often barrel-shaped to globular through curving of prism faces, acicular, tabular to thick tabular, as reniform crusts, radiating fibrous aggregates, earthy.
Occurrence: In the oxidation zone of lead deposits that also bear arsenic-containing minerals. Often in association with pyromorphite, with which it also forms mixed crystals ("campylite"). While pyromorphite usually occurs only in the uppermost zones, mimetite can also appear in deeper deposit regions.
Associated Minerals: Galena, cerussite, duftite, anglesite, wulfenite.
Similar Minerals: Apatite is harder. Vanadinite and pyromorphite are indistinguishable by ordinary methods, but the paragenesis with arsenic-containing minerals is indicative.

White Streak

1 Sainfeldite, Richelsdorf (Hesse, Germany), 5x

2 Edingtonite, Ice River (Canada), 3x

3 Epistilbite, Osilo (Sardinia, Italy), 4x

4 Heulandite, Habachtal (Austria), 8x

1 Sainfeldite
Hardness: 4.
Density: 3.0.
Streak: White.
Chemical Formula:
$H_2Ca_6(AsO_4)_4 \cdot H_2O$
Color: Colorless, white,
pink; vitreous luster.
Cleavage: None; fracture
uneven.
Tenacity: Brittle.
Crystal Form: Monoclinic;
prismatic, thick tabular, as
rosettes.
Occurrence: In the oxidation
zone.
Associated Minerals:
Pharmacolite, guerinite,
picropharmacolite.

Similar Minerals:
Pharmacolite and guerinite
have a perfect cleavage.

2 Edingtonite
Hardness: 4.
Density: 2.8.
Streak: White.
Chemical Formula:
$BaAl_2Si_3O_{10} \cdot 4H_2O$
Color: Colorless, white;
vitreous luster.
Cleavage: Perfect; fracture
uneven.
Tenacity: Brittle.
Crystal Form:
Orthorhombic; prismatic,
massive.
Occurrence: In cavities in

volcanic rocks.
Associated Minerals:
Heulandite, stilbite,
manganite.
Similar Minerals: Stilbite,
harmotome, and phillipsite
have a different crystal form.

3 Epistilbite
Hardness: 4.
Density: 2.25.
Streak: White.
Chemical Formula:
$CaAl_2Si_6O_{16} \cdot 5H_2O$
Color: Colorless, white,
reddish; vitreous luster.
Cleavage: Perfect; fracture
uneven.
Tenacity: Brittle.

5 Rhodochrosite, Peru, 3x

Because of its raspberry-red color, rhodochrosite is popularly known in Germany as "raspberry spar."

6 Rhodochrosite, Wolf Mine (Siegerland, Germany), 4x

Crystal Form: Monoclinic; prismatic, radiating fibrous.
Occurrence: In cavities in volcanic rocks.
Associated Minerals: Yugawaralite and stilbite have a different crystal form.

4 Heulandite
Hardness: $3^1/_2$–4.
Density: 2.2.
Streak: White.
Chemical Formula: $Ca[Al_2Si_7O_{18}] \cdot 6H_2O$
Color: Colorless, white, yellowish, red; vitreous luster, on cleavage surfaces pearly luster.
Cleavage: Highly perfect,

one cleavage face; fracture uneven.
Tenacity: Brittle.
Crystal Form: Monoclinic; thin to thick tabular, attached.
Occurrence: In druses of pegmatites, as lining in ore veins, in vesicles in volcanic rocks.
Associated Minerals: Stilbite, chabazite, scolecite.
Similar Minerals: Stilbite has a different crystal form.

5/6 Rhodochrosite
(See also photos 1 and 2, page 178)
Hardness: $3^1/_2$–4.
Density: 3.3–3.6.

Streak: White.
Chemical Formula: $MnCO_3$
Color: Rose-pink, light red, yellowish gray, brownish; vitreous luster.
Cleavage: Perfect rhombohedral; fracture uneven.
Tenacity: Brittle.
Crystal Form: Trigonal; often rounded, rhombohedrons, scalenohedrons, commonly globular, reniform, radiating fibrous, stalactitic, crusty.
Occurrence: In hydrothermal veins, in the oxidation zone, as lenticular particles and large deposits in metamorphic rocks.

177

2 Rhodochrosite, Siegerland (Germany), 3x

1 Rhodochrosite, Wolf Mine (Germany), 4x

3 Dolomite, Siegerland (Germany), 1x

Associated Minerals: Rhodonite, quartz, limonite, pyrolusite.

Similar Minerals: Calcite effervesces with cold dilute hydrochloric acid. Sometimes rhodochrosite is indistinguishable from manganese-containing dolomite by ordinary methods.

3 Dolomite
Hardness: 3½–4.
Density: 2.85–2.95.
Streak: White.
Chemical Formula: $CaMg(CO_3)_2$
Color: Colorless, white, gray, brownish, blackish; vitreous luster.
Cleavage: Perfect rhombohedral; fracture sparry.
Tenacity: Brittle.
Crystal Form: Trigonal; usually only in rhombohedrons, often curved in a saddle shape, very rarely with more faces, often massive.
Occurrence: In hydrothermal veins as a gangue mineral and in druses, rock-forming, crystals commonly lining fissures in dolomite rocks.

Associated Minerals: Quartz, calcite, and many others.

Special Property: Effervesces only with hot hydrochloric acid.

Similar Minerals: Calcite effervesces with cold dilute hydrochloric acid. Quartz is harder; gypsum is softer. Anhydrite has a different cleavage and also does not effervesce with hot hydrochloric acid.

4 Magnesite, Austria, 0.2x

5 Magnesite, Brazil, 0.5x

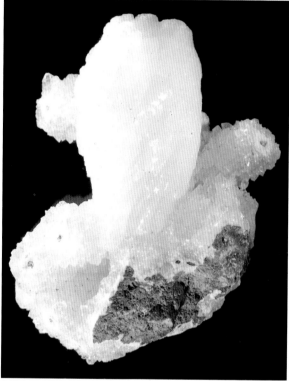

6 Goosecreekite, Poona (India), 4x

4/5 Magnesite
Hardness: 4–4¹/₂.
Density: 3.0.
Streak: White.
Chemical Formula: $MgCO_3$
Color: Colorless, white,
yellowish, brownish, gray;
vitreous luster.
Cleavage: Highly perfect
rhombohedral; fracture sparry.
Tenacity: Brittle.
Crystal Form: Trigonal;
rarely rhombohedral, usually
massive, granular, sparry
aggregates.
Occurrence: Large replacement bodies in dolomites, in
talc schists, lining fissures in
serpentine.

Associated Minerals:
Aragonite, calcite, dolomite.
Similar Minerals: Calcite
effervesces even with cold,
dilute hydrochloric acid.
Dolomite is somewhat softer,
but is often indistinguishable
from magnesite by ordinary
methods.

6 Goosecreekite
Hardness: 4–4¹/₂.
Density: 2.45.
Streak: White.
Chemical Formula:
$CaAl_2Si_6O_{16} \cdot 5H_2O$
Color: Colorless, white;
vitreous luster.
Cleavage: Not discernible;

fracture uneven.
Tenacity: Brittle.
Crystal Form: Monoclinic;
prismatic.
Occurrence: In cavities in
volcanic rocks.
Associated Minerals:
Quartz, epistilbite.
Similar Minerals: The
characteristic developmental
form distinguishes goose-
creekite from all similar
minerals.

179

1 Fluorite, Göschenen (Switzerland), 0.5x

3 Fluorite, China, 2x

2 Fluorite, Spain, 1x

4 Fluorite, Spain, 4x

1/2/3/4 Fluorite

Hardness: 4.
Density: 3.1–3.2.
Streak: White.
Chemical Formula: CaF_2
Color: Colorless, white, pink, yellow, brown, green, blue, violet, sometimes also several colors in one crystal; vitreous luster.
Cleavage: Perfect octahedral; fracture uneven.
Tenacity: Brittle.
Crystal Form: Isometric; cubes, octahedrons, also in combination with each other or with other crystal forms, radiated, reniform, massive.
Occurrence: In hydrothermal veins and druses in chalks, fissures in silicate rocks, layered in sedimentary rocks.
Associated Minerals: Calcite, barite, quartz, ore minerals.
Similar Minerals: Fluorite is distinguished from apatite by its crystal form and cleavage, from calcite and quartz by its hardness. Halite is soluble in water and tastes salty.

5 Phillipsite

Hardness: 4–4¹/₂.
Density: 2.2.
Streak: White.
Chemical Formula: $KCa[Al_3Si_5O_{16}] \cdot 6H_2O$
Color: Colorless, white, yellowish, reddish; vitreous luster.
Cleavage: Distinct; fracture uneven.
Tenacity: Brittle.
Crystal Form: Monoclinic; very rarely single, usually twins and fourlings, radiating fibrous, globular, almost always attached.
Occurrence: In vesicles in volcanic rocks.

5 Phillipsite, Siegerland (Germany), 4x

6 Yugawaralite, India, 3x

Fluorite is one of the most varicolored minerals in existence. It occurs in all hues, and sometimes it even has two or more colors.

7 Gmelinite, Siegerland (Germany), 2x

Associated Minerals: Chabazite, natrolite.
Similar Minerals: Stilbite and heulandite have a perfect cleavage, with a pearly luster on the cleavage surfaces.

6 Yugawaralite
Hardness: 4¹/₂.
Density: 2.25.
Streak: White.
Chemical Formula: $CaAl_2Si_6O_{16} \cdot 4H_2O$
Color: Colorless, white; vitreous luster.
Cleavage: Poor; fracture uneven.
Tenacity: Brittle.
Crystal Form: Monoclinic; tabular.
Occurrence: In cavities in volcanic rocks.
Associated Minerals: Quartz, heulandite.
Similar Minerals: Epistilbite has a different crystal form and perfect cleavage.

7 Gmelinite
Hardness: 4¹/₂.
Density: 2.1.
Streak: White.
Chemical Formula: $(Na_2,Ca)Al_2Si_4O_{12} \cdot 6H_2O$
Color: Colorless, white, pink, yellowish; vitreous luster.
Cleavage: None; fracture uneven.
Tenacity: Brittle.
Crystal Form: Hexagonal; thick tabular, bipyramidal.
Occurrence: In cavities in volcanic rocks.
Associated Minerals: Phillipsite, chabazite.
Similar Minerals: Considering the characteristic crystal form of gmelinite, no misidentification is possible.

1 Kyanite, Alpe Sponda (Ticino, Switzerland), 2x

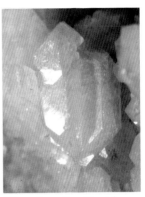

2 Harmotome, Harz Mountains (Germany), 6x

Kyanite is the only mineral in which the directional difference in hardness can be easily determined by ordinary methods.

1 Kyanite
(Disthene, Cyanite)
Hardness: 4–4¹/₂ parallel to length of crystals, 6–7 at right angles to that.
Density: 3.6–3.7.
Streak: White.
Chemical Formula: $Al_2[O/SiO_4]$
Color: Blue, gray, whitish; vitreous luster.
Cleavage: Perfect; fracture uneven.
Tenacity: Brittle.
Crystal Form: Triclinic; bladed, radiating fibrous, always embedded.
Occurrence: In metamorphic rocks, gneisses, and mica schists.
Associated Minerals: Staurolite, quartz, mica.
Similar Minerals: Kyanite is distinguished from all other minerals by different hardness in different directions.

2 Harmotome
Hardness: 4¹/₂.
Density: 2.44–2.50.
Streak: White.
Chemical Formula: $Ba[Al_2Si_6O_{16}] \cdot 6H_2O$
Color: Colorless, white, yellowish; vitreous luster.
Cleavage: Barely discernible; fracture conchoidal.
Tenacity: Brittle.
Crystal Form: Monoclinic; almost always penetration twins, attached.
Occurrence: In cavities in volcanic rocks, in hydrothermal complements and pyrite deposits.
Associated Minerals: Stilbite, heulandite, brewsterite, barite.
Similar Minerals: Harmotome cannot be distinguished from phillipsite by ordinary methods, but the latter seldom appears in ore deposits.

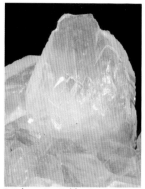

3 Colemanite, California, 3x

4 Wollastonite, Saxony (Ger.), 2x

5 Legrandite, Mapimi (Mexico), 3x

3 Colemanite
Hardness: 4¹/₂.
Density: 2.4.
Streak: White.
Chemical Formula:
$Ca[B_3O_4(OH)_3] \cdot H_2O$
Color: Colorless, white;
vitreous luster.
Cleavage: Perfect; fracture
uneven.
Tenacity: Brittle.
Crystal Form: Monoclinic;
prismatic, granular, massive.
Occurrence: In borax lake
bed deposits and sediments.
Associated Minerals:
Realgar, hydroboracite.
Similar Minerals: Borax is
softer.

4 Wollastonite
Hardness: 4¹/₂–5.
Density: 2.8–2.9.
Streak: White.
Chemical Formula:
$Ca_3[Si_3O_9]$
Color: Colorless, white,
gray; vitreous luster.
Cleavage: Perfect; fracture
fibrous.
Tenacity: Brittle.
Crystal Form: Triclinic;
rarely tabular, fibrous,
radiated.
Occurrence: In metamorphic
limestones.
Associated Minerals:
Grossular, vesuvianite.
Similar Minerals: Tremolite

is harder.

5 Legrandite
Hardness: 4¹/₂.
Density: 4.0.
Streak: White.
Chemical Formula:
$Zn_2(OH)AsO_4 \cdot H_2O$
Color: Colorless, yellow;
vitreous luster.
Cleavage: Poor; uneven.
Tenacity: Brittle.
Crystal Form: Monoclinic;
prismatic, radiated.
Occurrence: Oxidation zone.
Associated Minerals:
Limonite, adamite, mimetite.
Similar Minerals: Adamite
has a different crystal form.

White Streak

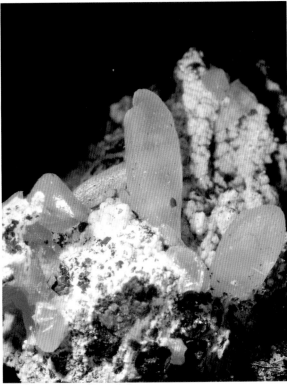

1 Smithsonite, Lavrion (Greece), 4x

2 Smithsonite, Tsumeb (Namibia), 6x

3 Whiteite, Canada, 2x

1/2 Smithsonite
Hardness: 5.
Density: 4.3–4.5.
Streak: White.
Chemical Formula:
$ZnCO_3$
Color: Colorless, white, yellow, brown, red, green, blue, gray; vitreous luster.
Cleavage: Perfect rhombohedral; fracture uneven.
Tenacity: Brittle.
Crystal Form: Trigonal; scalenohedrons and rhombohedrons, often rounded, reniform, stalactitic, lamellated, massive.
Occurrence: In the oxidation zone.

Associated Minerals: Hydrozincite, wulfenite, hemimorphite, aurichalcite.
Similar Minerals: Calcite, unlike smithsonite, effervesces with dilute hydrochloric acid.

3 Whiteite
Hardness: 4.
Density: 2.6.
Streak: White.
Chemical Formula:
$Ca(Fe,Mn)Mg_2Al_2(OH)_2(H_2O)_8(PO_4)_4$
Color: Brown; vitreous luster.
Cleavage: Perfect; fracture uneven.
Tenacity: Brittle.

Crystal Form: Monoclinic; thick tabular, prismatic.
Occurrence: In phosphate deposits.
Associated Minerals: Lazulite, siderite.
Similar Minerals: Siderite has a different crystal form.

4 Apophyllite
Hardness: 4½–5.
Density: 2.3–2.4.
Streak: White.
Chemical Formula:
$KCa_4[(F,OH)/(Si_4O_{10})_2] \cdot 8H_2O$
Color: Colorless, white, yellow, green, brown, pink; vitreous luster, on the basal

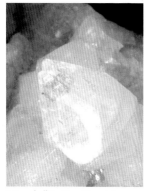

4 Apophyllite, Harz Mountains (Germany), 3x

Although the crystals of chabazite look almost like cubes, they are actually trigonal rhombohedrons.

5 Chabazite, Stzgeom (Poland), 4x

face strong pearly luster.
Cleavage: Perfect basal; fracture uneven.
Tenacity: Brittle.
Crystal Form: Tetragonal; tabular, pseudocubic, prismatic, also bipyramidal, lamellar, granular, coarse.
Occurrence: In vesicles in volcanic rocks, in druses and lining fissures in ore veins or cavities in silicate rock.
Associated Minerals: Stilbite, heulandite.
Similar Minerals: Apophyllite is distinguished from all other minerals of this paragenesis by its crystal form and luster.

5 Chabazite
Hardness: $4^{1}/_{2}$.
Density: 2.08.
Streak: White.
Chemical Formula: $Ca[Al_2Si_4O_{12}]$
Color: Colorless, white, yellow, orange, brown; vitreous luster.
Cleavage: Indistinct; fracture uneven.
Tenacity: Brittle.
Crystal Form: Trigonal; pseudocubic rhombohedrons, often in twins, always attached.
Occurrence: In vesicles in volcanic rocks and cavities in pegmatites, in druses and

fissures in ore veins.
Associated Minerals: Stilbite, heulandite, scolecite, natrolite.
Similar Minerals: Calcite is distinguished from chabazite by its cleavage, and it effervesces with dilute hydrochloric acid. Fluorite also has a distinct cleavage.

1 Hemimorphite, Mapimi (Mexico), 4x

2 Scheelite, Rauris (Austria), 3x

3 Scheelite, Saxony (Germany), 3x

1 Hemimorphite
Hardness: 5.
Density: 3.3–3.5.
Streak: White.
Chemical Formula:
$Zn_4[(OH)_2/Si_2O_7] \cdot H_2O$
Color: Colorless, white, greenish, brown, yellowish; vitreous luster.
Cleavage: Perfect; fracture conchoidal.
Tenacity: Brittle.
Crystal Form: Orthorhombic; prismatic to acicular, tabular, radiated, reniform, stalactitic, crusty.
Occurrence: In the oxidation zone.
Associated Minerals: Smithsonite, hydrozincite, aurichalcite.
Similar Minerals: Barite is distinctly heavier.

2/3 Scheelite
Hardness: 4¹/₂–5.
Density: 5.9–6.1.
Streak: White.
Chemical Formula: $CaWO_4$
Color: Colorless, white, yellowish gray, orange, brown; greasy luster.
Cleavage: Difficult to discern; fracture conchoidal.
Tenacity: Brittle.
Crystal Form: Tetragonal; usually bipyramids, rarely with base, often massive, granular.
Occurrence: In pegmatites, pneumatolytic veins, hydrothermal gold ore veins, contact metamorphic deposits.
Associated Minerals: Fluorite, cassiterite, wolframite.
Special Property: Intensely fluorescent.
Similar Minerals: Anatase does not fluoresce and has a different luster. Fluorite has perfect octahedral cleavage.

4 Apatite, Kola Peninsula (Russia), 2x

6 Apatite, Pakistan, 1x

5 Apatite, Knappenwand (Austria), 6x

7 Childrenite, Brazil, 2x

4/5/6 Apatite
Hardness: 5.
Density: 3.16–3.22.
Streak: White.
Chemical Formula:
$Ca_5[(F,Cl)/(PO_4)_3]$
Color: Colorless, yellow, blue, green, violet, red; vitreous luster.
Cleavage: Sometimes distinct basal; fracture conchoidal.
Tenacity: Brittle.
Crystal Form: Hexagonal; prismatic, long to short columnar, occasionally globular owing to numerous faces, acicular, also massive, attached and embedded.
Occurrence: Microscopic in all igneous rocks, in pegmatites and hydrothermal veins, as concretions and beds in sediments.
Associated Minerals: Magnetite, anatase, rutile, leucite.
Similar Minerals: Quartz, beryl, phenakite, and milarite are harder; calcite, pyromorphite, and mimetite are softer.

7 Childrenite
Hardness: 4¹/₂.
Density: 3.0.
Streak: White.
Chemical Formula:
$(Fe,Mn)Al[(OH)_2/PO_4] \cdot H_2O$
Color: Yellow to brown; vitreous luster.
Cleavage: Usually not discernible; fracture conchoidal.
Tenacity: Brittle.
Crystal Form: Monoclinic; prismatic, radiating fibrous.
Occurrence: In phosphate pegmatites.
Associated Minerals: Quartz, feldspar.
Similar Minerals: Laueite has a different crystal form.

187

1 Analcime, Rossbach (Bavaria, Germany), 2x

3 Thomsonite, Tenerife (Canary Islands), 6x

2 Thomsonite, Saxony (Germany), 8x

4 Carpholite, Harz Mountains (Germany), 2x

1 Analcime
Hardness: 5½.
Density: 2.2–2.3.
Streak: White.
Chemical Formula:
$Na[AlSi_2O_6] \cdot H_2O$
Color: Colorless, white,
reddish, orange, yellow;
vitreous luster.
Cleavage: Indistinct; fracture
conchoidal.
Tenacity: Brittle.
Crystal Form: Isometric;
almost exclusively in deltoid
ikositetrahedrons, also
massive, usually attached.
Occurrence: In vesicles in
volcanic rocks, in ore veins,
also embedded in syenites

and basalts.
Associated Minerals:
Calcite, apophyllite, quartz,
zeolites.
Similar Minerals: Leucite in
attached crystals is
indistinguishable by ordinary
methods.

2/3 Thomsonite
Hardness: 5–5½.
Density: 2.3–2.4.
Streak: White.
Chemical Formula:
$NaCa_2[Al_5Si_5O_{20}] \cdot 6H_2O$
Color: Colorless, white;
vitreous luster.
Cleavage: Perfect; fracture
uneven.

Tenacity: Brittle.
Crystal Form:
Orthorhombic; prismatic,
tabular, radiating fibrous,
fibrous.
Occurrence: In vesicles in
volcanic rocks.
Associated Minerals:
Natrolite, chabazite,
phillipsite.
Similar Minerals: Natrolite
crystals are square in cross
section, but often not easily
distinguished from
thomsonite.

5 Titanite, Pakistan, 1x

Because of their wedge-shaped development, titanite crystals are also known as sphene. (In Greek, sphēn = wedge.)

6 Titanite, Dodo (Urals, Russia), 6x

4 Carpholite
Hardness: 5–5^1/$_2$.
Density: 3.0.
Streak: White.
Chemical Formula: $MnAl_2Si_2O_6(OH)_4$
Color: Straw-yellow; vitreous luster.
Cleavage: Perfect; fracture fibrous.
Tenacity: Brittle.
Crystal Form: Orthorhombic; fibrous, radiating fibrous.
Occurrence: In hydrothermal veins, in tin deposits.
Associated Minerals: Quartz, fluorite.
Similar Minerals: The color and crystal form make this mineral unmistakable.

5/6 Titanite
(Sphene)
Hardness: 5–5^1/$_2$.
Density: 3.4–6.
Streak: White.
Chemical Formula: $CaTi[O/SiO_4]$
Color: Colorless, white, yellow, greenish, red, brown, blackish brown, blue; resinous luster.
Cleavage: Difficult to discern; fracture conchoidal.
Tenacity: Brittle.
Crystal Form: Monoclinic; tabular to prismatic, often penetration twins with reentrant angles.
Occurrence: Embedded in many igneous rocks and crystalline schists, pegmatites, marbles.
Associated Minerals: Quartz, feldspar, anatase, rutile, calcite.
Similar Minerals: Anatase is distinctly tetragonal. Monazite has a green glow in unfiltered UV light.

White Streak

2 Natrolite, Saxony (Germany), 3x

Because of their acicular crystals, natrolite and scolecite belong to the group of so-called needle zeolites.

1 Scolecite, Hollersbachtal (Austria), 4x

1 Scolecite
Hardness: 5¹/₂.
Density: 2.26–2.40.
Streak: White.
Chemical Formula: $Ca[Al_2Si_3O_{10}] \cdot 3H_2O$
Color: Colorless, white; vitreous luster.
Cleavage: Perfect, but hard to discern in acicular crystals; fracture conchoidal.
Tenacity: Brittle.
Crystal Form: Monoclinic; acicular to prismatic, radiating fibrous.
Occurrence: In fissures in granites and syenites, in vesicles in volcanic rocks.
Associated Minerals: Apophyllite, laumontite, stilbite, heulandite.
Similar Minerals: Natrolite generally has finer fibers and tends to be limited to volcanic rocks; otherwise it is virtually indistinguishable from scolecite by ordinary methods.

2 Natrolite
Hardness: 5–5¹/₂.
Density: 2.2–2.4.
Streak: White.
Chemical Formula: $Na_2[Al_2Si_3O_{10}] \cdot 2H_2O$
Color: Colorless, white, yellow; vitreous luster.
Cleavage: Perfect, but not discernible because of the development; fracture conchoidal.
Tenacity: Brittle.
Crystal Form: Orthorhombic; prismatic to acicular, as fibrous crusts.
Occurrence: In vesicles in volcanic rocks, in syenites and nepheline syenites.
Associated Minerals: Phillipsite, analcime, chabazite.
Similar Minerals: Scolecite, though hard to distinguish from natrolite, is scarcer and often is found in a different paragenesis. Thomsonite has a different crystal form.

190

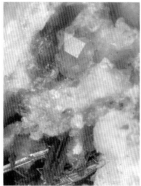

3 Monazite, Gasteiner Tal (Austria), 10x

4 Hureaulite, Portugal, 6x

In contrast to the dark, opaque monazite from pegmatites, the monazite found in Alpine cavities is always light in color and translucent to transparent.

5 Hureaulite, Portugal, 8x

3 Monazite

Hardness: 5–5¹/₂.
Density: 4.9–5.5.
Streak: White.
Chemical Formula: $CePO_4$
Color: Colorless, orange, transparent brown, opaque brown to dark brown; vitreous to greasy luster.
Cleavage: Sometimes visible; fracture conchoidal.
Tenacity: Brittle.
Crystal Form: Monoclinic; thick tabular to prismatic, more rarely massive, attached and embedded.
Occurrence: Microscopically distributed in igneous rocks, in pegmatites and placers.
Associated Minerals: Quartz, feldspar, xenotime.
Similar Minerals: Titanite has a different crystal form.

4/5 Hureaulite

Hardness: 5.
Density: 3.2.
Streak: White.
Chemical Formula: $(Mn,Fe)_5H_2[PO_4]_4 \cdot 4H_2O$
Color: Pink, reddish, brownish, yellow, white, colorless; vitreous luster.
Cleavage: None; fracture uneven.
Tenacity: Brittle.
Crystal Form: Monoclinic; prismatic, with slanted pinacoid faces, radiated, massive.
Occurrence: In phosphate pegmatites.
Associated Minerals: Rockbridgeite, phosphoferrite, reddingite.
Similar Minerals: Strengite has a different crystal form.

191

White Streak

1 Anatase, Rauris (Austria), 10x

3 Brookite, Eicham (Austria), 3x

2 Anatase, Brazil, 10x

4 Leucite, Tuscany (Italy), 2x

1/2 Anatase
Hardness: 5½–6.
Density: 3.8–3.9.
Streak: White.
Chemical Formula: TiO_2
Color: Colorless, pink, red, yellow, blue, brown, black, green; metallic to adamantine luster.
Cleavage: Usually not visible; fracture uneven.
Tenacity: Brittle.
Crystal Form: Tetragonal; steep to shallow bipyramids, tabular, almost always attached, often horizontally striated.
Occurrence: As fissure or vein deposits.

Associated Minerals: Brookite, rutile, titanite.
Similar Minerals: Magnetite and hematite have a different streak. Brookite has a different crystal form.

3 Brookite
Hardness: 5½–6.
Density: 4.1.
Streak: Light brown to white.
Chemical Formula: TiO_2
Color: Brown, greenish to blackish; adamantine luster.
Cleavage: Indistinct; fracture uneven.
Tenacity: Brittle.

Crystal Form: Orthorhombic; thin tabular, rarely pseudohexagonal bipyramids.
Occurrence: As fissure or vein deposits, in cavities in alkali rocks.
Associated Minerals: Anatase, rutile, quartz, feldspar, hematite, titanite.
Similar Minerals: Hematite has a different streak. Anatase is always distinctly tetragonal.

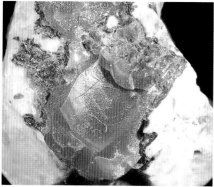

5 Fire opal, Querétaro (Mexico), 2x

6 Precious opal, Yowah (Australia), 0.5x

Opal, like quartz, is silicon dioxide. Unlike crystalline quartz, however, opal has no ordered crystal lattice; it is amorphous.

7 Precious opal, Yowah (Australia), 2x

4 Leucite

Hardness: $5^1/_2$–6.
Density: 2.5.
Streak: White.
Chemical Formula:
$KAlSi_2O_6$
Color: Colorless, white; vitreous luster.
Cleavage: None; fracture uneven.
Tenacity: Brittle.
Crystal Form: Tetragonal, pseudoisometric; deltoid ikositetrahedrons, almost always embedded.
Occurrence: In volcanic rocks.
Associated Minerals: Augite, biotite.

Similar Minerals: Analcime is usually attached, but otherwise difficult to distinguish.

5/6/7 Opal
Hardness: 5–$6^1/_2$.
Density: 1.9–2.2.
Streak: White.
Chemical Formula: $SiO_2 \cdot nH_2O$
Color: Colorless, transparent (hyalite), whitish, bluish with a play of rainbow colors (precious opal), red to orange, translucent (fire opal), green, red, brown, yellow, opaque (common opal); waxy to vitreous luster.
Cleavage: None; fracture conchoidal.
Tenacity: Brittle.
Crystal Form: Amorphous; massive, embedded.
Occurrence: In cavities in volcanic rocks, in sediments at the level of the groundwater table, as a deposit from hot springs (geyserite).
Associated Minerals: Zeolites, chalcedony.
Similar Minerals: Chalcedony can resemble opal, but is indistinguishable by ordinary methods. Precious opal is distinguished by its brilliant play of colors.

193

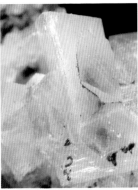

2 Adularia, Pakistan, 4x

3 Amazonite, Brazil, 0.5x

1 Potassium feldspar twin, Baveno (Italy), 8x

1/2/3 Potassium Feldspars

Hardness: 6.
Density: 2.53–2.56.
Streak: White.
Chemical Formula:
$K[AlSi_3O_8]$

Two modifications exist:
monoclinic orthoclase,
formed at high temperatures,
and triclinic microcline,
formed at low temperatures.
Clear potassium feldspar
formed at high temperatures
from volcanic rocks is known
as sanidine.

Adularia, a potassium
feldspar of hydrothermal
origin, is distinguished by its
distinctive form.

Amazonite is a green
feldspar of pegmatitic origin.
Color: Colorless, white,
yellow, brown, flesh-colored,
green; vitreous luster.
Cleavage: Perfect parallel to
the base, less perfect parallel
to the side pinacoid; fracture
conchoidal.
Tenacity: Brittle.
Crystal Form: Monoclinic
(orthoclase) and triclinic
(microcline); prismatic,
tabular, also rhombohedral
(adularia), often twinned,
often massive in large
aggregates.
Occurrence: In granites,
syenites, trachytes, rhyolites,
gneisses, arkoses, graywack-
es, pegmatites, hydrothermal
veins.
Associated Minerals:
Quartz, muscovite, biotite,
plagioclase, garnet,
tourmaline.
Similar Minerals: Quartz
has no cleavage. Calcite,
barite, gypsum, and dolomite
are softer. Plagioclase has a
different crystal form.

White Streak

4 Albite, Bavaria (Germany), 1x

6 Pericline, Rauris (Austria), 1x

5 Albite, Switzerland, 8x

4/5/6 Plagioclase

Hardness: 6–6½.
Density: 2.61–2.77.
Streak: White.

The plagioclases form a solid solution series with the end members.

Chemical Formula:
$Na[AlSi_3O_8]$ and $Ca[Al_2Si_2O_8]$. The names of the intermediate members of the series vary with the change in chemical composition:

Albite	90–100% albite
Oligoclase	70–90% albite
Andesine	50–70% albite
Labradorite	30–50% albite
Bytownite	10–30% albite
Anorthite	0–10% albite

Distinguishing among the individual members is usually not possible by ordinary methods.

Color: Colorless, white, greenish, reddish, gray; vitreous luster.

Cleavage: Perfect basal cleavage, less perfect parallel to the side pinacoid; fracture conchoidal.

Tenacity: Brittle.

Crystal Form: Triclinic; prismatic to tabular, commonly twinned; the twinned, porcelain-white plagioclase found in Alpine cavities is called pericline; commonly massive.

Occurrence: In granites, gabbros, anorthosites, in gneisses, granulites, pegmatites, lining Alpine cavities, lining fissures in ore veins.

Associated Minerals: Potassium feldspar, quartz, biotite, muscovite.

Similar Minerals: Quartz has no cleavage. Calcite, barite, gypsum, and dolomite are softer. Potassium feldspar has different crystal forms, although when massive it is generally hard to distinguish by ordinary methods.

195

2 Andalusite, Lisens (Austria), 2x

1 Axinite, Switzerland, 8x

3 Andalusite, Spain, 2x

1 Axinite
Hardness: 6¹/₂–7.
Density: 3.3.
Streak: White.
Chemical Formula:
$Ca_2(Fe,Mg,Mn)Al_2$
$[OH/BO_3/Si_4O_{12}]$
Color: Brown, gray, violet,
blue, greenish; vitreous luster.
Cleavage: Poorly visible;
fracture conchoidal.
Tenacity: Brittle.
Crystal Form: Triclinic;
tabular, very sharp-edged,
usually attached, massive,
sparry, bladed.
Occurrence: In calcium
silicate rocks and contact
metasomatic deposits, in
druses in pegmatites.
Associated Minerals:
Clinozoisite, chlorite, apatite.
Similar Minerals: The
sharp-edged crystals of
axinite are unmistakable.

2/3 Andalusite
(Chiastolite)
Hardness: 7.
Density: 3.1–3.2.
Streak: White.
Chemical Formula:
$Al_2[O/SiO_4]$
Color: Various shades of
gray, yellowish, reddish,
green, brown, sometimes also
multicolored; vitreous luster,
but usually dull-surfaced.
Cleavage: Usually indistinct;
fracture uneven.
Tenacity: Brittle.
Crystal Form:
Orthorhombic; thick columnar
with almost square cross
section, radiating fibrous,
almost always embedded.
Occurrence: In gneisses and
mica schists, in hard quartz in
metamorphic rocks, in clay
schists and pegmatites.
Associated Minerals:
Quartz, feldspar, tourmaline,
mica.
Similar Minerals:
Tourmaline has a different
crystal form, with a three- or
six-sided cross section.

4 Melanophlogite, Livorno (Italy), 3x

Spodumene displays extremely
intense pleochroism. That is, when
observed from different sides, it
reveals different colors ranging
from yellow to violet.

5 Spodumene, Afghanistan, 0.5x

Hornblende, augite, and actinolite have a different cleavage.

4 Melanophlogite
Hardness: 6¹/₂–7.
Density: 2.0.
Streak: White.
Chemical Formula: SiO_2
Color: Colorless, white; vitreous luster.
Cleavage: None; fracture conchoidal.
Tenacity: Brittle.
Crystal Form: Isometric; cubes, globular.
Occurrence: In sedimentary rocks.
Associated Minerals: Sulfur, calcite.
Similar Minerals: Fluorite and calcite are much softer.

5 Spodumene
Hardness: 6¹/₂–7.
Density: 3.1–3.2.
Streak: White.
Chemical Formula: $LiAl[Si_2O_6]$
Color: Colorless, white, pink, and lilac (kunzite), green (hiddenite), yellow, brown.
Cleavage: Perfect prismatic; fracture sparry.
Tenacity: Brittle.
Crystal Form: Monoclinic; tabular, more rarely prismatic, radiated, sparry, massive, embedded and attached.
Occurrence: In pegmatites, embedded and dull; in druses in these pegmatites, transparent and beautifully colored.
Associated Minerals: Feldspar, quartz, beryl.
Similar Minerals: Feldspar has a different cleavage.

2 Smoky quartz, Habachtal (Austria), 1x

The golden-yellow acicular and capillary inclusions of rutile in quartz have always fascinated people. Owing to the beauty of rutilated quartz, in Germany this variety is also known as Venus hair.

1 Rose quartz crystals perched on feldspar, Minas Gerais (Brazil), 1x

1–10 Quartz
(See also pages 200–201)
Hardness: 7.
Density: 2.65.
Streak: White.
Chemical Formula: SiO_2
Color: Colorless or in a large range of colors (see under Varieties). Vitreous to greasy luster.
Cleavage: None; fracture conchoidal.
Tenacity: Brittle.
Crystal Form: Trigonal. High quartz (beta quartz), formed above 1063°F (573°C), is hexagonal; beta quartz crystals are pseudomorphs of low (trigonal) quartz after the hexagonal modification. The crystals are usually six-sided; distinctly trigonal (three-sided) crystals are formed at particularly low temperatures. Both right-handed and left-handed forms exist, often twinned types as well (for example, Japanese-law-twins with reentrant angles).

Crystals may be distorted and platy, acicular, short prismatic, or bipyramidal. Aggregates are radiating fibrous (star quartz), bladed, or granular.

Occurrence: As component of plutonic rocks (e.g., granite), volcanic rocks (e.g., rhyolite and quartz porphyry), sedimentary rocks (e.g., sandstone), and metamorphic rocks (e.g., gneiss).

Beautiful crystals are found lining druses in pegmatites, in pneumatolytic veins, in ore veins, in cavities in marble, in septaria, and embedded in sedimentary rocks.

3 Citrine crystal, Val d'Aosta (It.), 1x

4 Amethyst crystal, Brazil, 1x

5 Rock crystal, Corinto (Brazil), 1.5x

Associated Minerals:
Limestone, feldspar, ores, tourmaline, garnet, and many others.

Varieties: Quartz is an extremely common mineral that can occur in many different varieties. Some of them—amethyst, rose quartz, rock crystal, or smoky quartz, for example—are used to make jewelry because of their beautiful colors.

Rock crystal is colorless, clear, and transparent. Its crystals are found within fissures in sandstones, cavities in marbles, and druses in pegmatites (where they usually are not particularly clear, however). In cavities in ore veins, rock crystal is associated with ore minerals, with the clear varieties often being more recent than the ore minerals.

In septaria (more or less round to loaf-shaped, hard concretions traversed by a network of cracks) are found superb, shiny rock crystals, which are often popularly known as "diamonds"—depending on the site, as Mirabeau diamonds (France), Herkimer diamonds (Herkimer, NY), or Marmaroscher diamonds. Such rock crystals often have inclusions of substances such as petroleum. Most Japanese-law-twins are also rock crystals; quartz varieties of a different color with this type of twinning are extremely rare.

Smoky quartz is the name given to quartz of a smoky brown to dark brown color. Deep black smoky quartz is also known as morion. The color results from exposure to

7 Rutilated quartz, Itabira (Brazil), 2x

6 Quartz, Serifos (Greece), 2x

natural radioactivity; it disappears when the crystals are heated to several hundred degrees. Smoky quartz crystals are found in druses in pegmatites and in ore veins. More rarely, doubly terminated quartz enclosed in sedimentary rocks can also be smoky brown in color. *Amethyst* is intensely violet in color. Vesicles in volcanic rocks are completely coated with short prismatic crystals. More rare are long prismatic amethyst crystals, which occur in cavities in volcanic rocks, but also in ore veins. *Citrine* rarely forms pale-yellow crystals in druses. Brown burnt amethyst is often falsely sold as citrine. *Rose quartz* is pink quartz from pegmatites, where it usually is massive. Crystals are extremely rare and usually not very large.

Ferruginous quartz is the term used for opaque quartz colored red by hematite inclusions. This form often occurs as a coating in ore veins and as inclusions in gypsum and clay rocks.

Milky quartz is quartz that is colored milky white by a large number of liquid inclusions. It usually occurs in massive form as a gangue mineral in hydrothermal veins. Less common are well-developed crystals such as those found in Alpine cavities. They are sometimes milky white only on the outside, while the inside is smoky brown or colorless.

Prase is an opaque quartz colored by inclusions of green minerals (e.g., heden-bergite); it normally appears

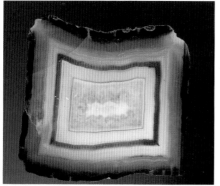

8 Agate. Brazil, 1x

9 Agate, St. Egidien (Saxony, Germany), 0.5x

10 Praseme, Serifos (Greece), 2x

only in massive form. Crystals of this color are sometimes found lining fissures in skarn rocks. *Chalcedony* is a microcrystalline quartz that forms reniform crusts filling cavities in volcanic rocks, more rarely also in ore veins or other rocks. It can occur in a wide variety of colors: Chalcedony in the narrower sense is gray to light blue in color, not often also with blue and white banding (banded chalcedony).

Red to reddish brown translucent chalcedony is called *carnelian*. The opaque brown to reddish brown, but also yellowish to greenish, variety is known as *jasper*. *Agate* is chalcedony that in different-colored concentric layers fills cavities in volcanic and other rocks. The layers may have a great variety of colors: Stones with alternating bands of black and white are known as *onyx*. Gray to brown nodules embedded in limestones are known as *flint* or *chert*.

Similar Minerals: Quartz is distinguished from other similar minerals by hardness and resistance to acid.

2 Tridymite, Italy, 4x

Tridymite crystals—unlike quartz, which has the same chemical composition— form only in cavities in volcanic rocks.

1 Spessartine on tourmaline, Pakistan, 2x

1 Spessartine
Hardness: 7.
Density: 4.19.
Streak: White.
Chemical Formula: $Mn_3Al_2[SiO_4]_3$
Color: Pink, orange, light brown to dark brown; vitreous luster.
Cleavage: None; fracture conchoidal.
Tenacity: Brittle.
Crystal Form: Isometric; deltoid icositetrahedrons, embedded and attached.
Occurrence: In metamorphic manganese deposits, in pegmatites and granites.
Associated Minerals: Rhodonite, feldspar, quartz.
Similar Minerals: Almandine is more reddish brown and, unlike spessartine, often displays rhombic dodecahedrons.

2 Tridymite
Hardness: 7.
Density: 2.27.
Streak: White.
Chemical Formula: SiO_2
Color: Colorless, white; vitreous luster.
Cleavage: Rarely visible; fracture conchoidal.
Tenacity: Brittle.
Crystal Form: Hexagonal when formed at high temperatures, upon cooling altered to the orthorhombic modification; tabular, in fan-shaped trillings, massive.
Occurrence: Lining fissures and in druses in acid volcanic rocks, in the contact zone of acid inclusions, in volcanic rocks.
Associated Minerals: High quartz, hornblende, pdeudobrookite, augite.
Similar Minerals: Sanidine usually is more thickly tabular and has a different crystal form. The typical paragenesis distinguishes tridymite from most other thin tabular white minerals.

3 Tourmaline, San Piero (Elba, Italy), 3x

5 Tourmaline, Brazil, 0.5x

4 Schorl, Horlberg (Bavaria, Germany), 1x

3/4/5 Tourmaline
Hardness: 7.
Density: 3.0–3.25.
Streak: White.
Chemical Formula: The tourmalines are a group of mixed crystals with the following major members:
Elbaite $Na(Li,Al)_3Al_6[(OH)_4/(BO_3)_3/Si_6O_{18}]$
Dravite $NaMg_3(Al,Fe^{+3})Al_6[(OH)_4/(BO_3)_3/Si_6O_{18}]$
Schorl $NaFe_3^{+2}(Al,Fe^{+3})_6[(OH)_4/(BO_3)_3/Si_6O_{18}]$
Buergerite $NaFe_3^{+3}Al_6[F/O_3(BO_3)_3/Si_6O_{18}]$
Tsilaisite $NaMn_3Al_6[(OH)_4/(BO_3)_3/Si_6O_{18}]$
Uvite $CaMg_3(Al_5Mg)$
$[(OH)_4/(BO_3)_3/Si_6O_{18}]$
Liddicoatite $Ca(Li,Al)_3Al_6[(OH)_4/(BO_3)_3/Si_6O_{18}]$
Color: Colorless, pink (rubellite), green (verdelite), blue (indigolite), yellow, brown, black, transparent to opaque; vitreous luster.
Cleavage: None; fracture conchoidal.
Tenacity: Brittle.
Crystal Form: Trigonal; prismatic to acicular, embedded and attached, radiated, bladed, massive.
Occurrence: In granites, pegmatites, pneumatolytic veins, hydrothermal veins, druses in pegmatites, mica schists and gneisses.
Associated Minerals: Quartz, feldspar, beryl, mica.
Similar Minerals: The usually distinctly three-sided cross section distinguishes tourmaline from all other minerals.

1 Almandine, Horlberg (Bavaria, Germany), 4x

2 Almandine, Zillertal (Austria), 1x

3 Grossular, Zillertal (Austria), 3x

1/2 Almandine
Hardness: $6^1/_2$–$7^1/_2$.
Density: 4.32.
Streak: White.
Chemical Formula: $Fe_3Al_2[SiO_4]_3$
Color: Red, sometimes with blue cast, reddish brown, brown; vitreous luster.
Cleavage: None; fracture conchoidal.
Tenacity: Brittle.
Crystal Form: Isometric; rhombic dodecahedrons and deltoid icositetrahedrons, almost always embedded.
Occurrence: In mica schists, gneisses, granulites, more rarely in pegmatites.
Associated Minerals: Staurolite, mica, quartz, feldspar.
Similar Minerals: The paragenesis of almandine in mica schists and gneisses is characteristic.

3 Grossular
Hardness: $6^1/_2$–7.
Density: 3.59.
Streak: White.
Chemical Formula: $Ca_3Al_2[SiO_4]_3$
Color: Colorless, yellow, yellowish brown, green, red (hessonite); vitreous luster.
Cleavage: None; fracture conchoidal.
Tenacity: Brittle.
Crystal Form: Isometric; deltoid icositetrahedrons and rhombic dodecahedrons, embedded and attached, massive.
Occurrence: In contact marbles, lining fissures in serpentinites.
Associated Minerals: Vesuvianite, diopside, calcite.
Similar Minerals: The paragenesis of grossular is quite characteristic. Vesuvianite is usually distinctly prismatic; when massive or in short prisms, it is hard to distinguish by ordinary methods.

4 Staurolite, Martelltal (South Tyrol, Italy), 0.5x

5 Androdite, Serifos (Greece), 2x

6 Andradite, Serifos (Greece), 1x

At one time the rectangular stauro-lite twins were often worn as a Christian symbol, because of their cruciform shape.

4 Staurolite
Hardness: 7–7$^1/_2$.
Density: 3.7–3.8.
Streak: White.
Chemical Formula: $(Fe,Mg,Zn)_2Al_9[O_6/(OH)_2/(SiO_4)_4]$
Color: Reddish brown to blackish brown; vitreous luster.
Cleavage: Barely visible; fracture conchoidal.
Tenacity: Brittle.
Crystal Form: Monoclinic; prismatic to tabular, often in cruciform twins (90° angle or about 60° angle between the arms), always embedded.

Occurrence: In mica schists and gneisses.
Associated Minerals: Quartz, mica, kyanite.
Similar Minerals: Tourmaline always has a distinct trigonal symmetry and never forms cruciform twins.

5/6 Andradite
Hardness: 6$^1/_2$–7$^1/_2$.
Density: 3.86.
Streak: White.
Chemical Formula: $Ca_3Fe_2[SiO_4]_3$
Color: Colorless, brown, green, black (melanite, titanium-containing andra-dite); vitreous luster.
Cleavage: None; fracture conchoidal.
Tenacity: Brittle.
Crystal Form: Isometric; rhombic dodecahedrons and deltoid icositetrahedrons, embedded and attached.
Occurrence: In metamorphic deposits, lining fissures in serpentines and skarn rocks, in volcanic rocks.
Associated Minerals: Chlorite, diopside, hedenbergite, magnetite.
Similar Minerals: Grossular is often indistinguishable from andradite by ordinary methods.

205

1 Boracite, Bernburg (Thuringia, Germany), 10x

2 Pyrope, Ticino (Switzerland), 1x

3 Pyrope, Bohemia
(Czechoslovakia), 0.5x

1 Boracite
Hardness: 7.
Density: 2.9–3.
Streak: White.
Chemical Formula:
$Mg_3[Cl/B_7O_{13}]$
Color: Colorless, white, yellowish, greenish, bluish; vitreous luster.
Cleavage: None; fracture conchoidal.
Tenacity: Brittle.
Crystal Form: Above 514°F (268°C) isometric, below that temperature orthorhombic; cubic, tetrahedral, embedded, massive, fibrous.
Occurrence: In salt deposits, where it is embedded in anhydrite or gypsum.
Associated Minerals: Gypsum, anhydrite, halite.
Similar Minerals: Halite is much softer and has a good cleavage; the same is true of fluorite.

2/3 Pyrope
Hardness: 7–7½.
Density: 3.58.
Streak: White.
Chemical Formula:
$Mg_3Al_2[SiO_4]$
Color: Dark red, blood-red, transparent; vitreous luster.
Cleavage: None; fracture conchoidal.
Tenacity: Brittle.
Crystal Form: Isometric; rhombic dodecahedrons, deltoid icositetrahedrons, often rounded grains, always embedded.
Occurrence: In ultrabasites, serpentinites, and placers.
Associated Minerals: Diamond, phlogopite, olivine.
Similar Minerals: The paragenesis of pyrope is characteristic. Almandine is always slightly more brownish, never pure dark red.

4 Olivine, Norway, 1x

5 Zircon, Pakistan, 2x

6 Zircon, Seiland (Norway), 1x

Beautifully colored transparent olivine is cut and polished for ornamental purposes. It then is called peridot.

4 Olivine
(Peridot)
Hardness: 7.
Density: 3.27–4.20.
Streak: White.
Chemical Formula: $(Mg,Fe)_2[SiO_4]$
Color: Yellowish green to bottle-green, red, brownish; vitreous luster, slightly greasy.
Cleavage: Barely discernible; fracture conchoidal.
Tenacity: Brittle.
Crystal Form: Orthorhombic; thick tabular to prismatic, often granular, massive.
Occurrence: In gabbros, diabases, basalts, peridotites, as lining of fissures in crystalline limestones, in meteorites.
Associated Minerals: Spinel, diopside, augite, hornblende.
Similar Minerals: Apatite is softer.

5/6 Zircon
Hardness: 7½.
Density: 4.55–4.67.
Streak: White.
Chemical Formula: $Zr[SiO_4]$
Color: Colorless, white, pink, yellow, green, blue, brown, brownish red; almost adamantine luster, on fracture surfaces greasy luster.
Cleavage: Barely discernible; fracture conchoidal.
Tenacity: Brittle.
Crystal Form: Tetragonal; prismatic to bipyramidal, attached, more commonly embedded.
Occurrence: In granites, syenites, rhyolites, trachytes, pyroclasts, placers, pegmatites.
Associated Minerals: Xenotime, monazite.
Similar Minerals: Vesuvianite is softer. Cassiterite is heavier.

1 Euclase, Zimbabwe, 4x

3 Aquamarine, Pakistan, 1x

2 Red beryl, Utah, 3x

4 Emerald, Habachtal (Austria), 2x

1 Euclase
Hardness: 7½.
Density: 3.0–3.1.
Streak: White.
Chemical Formula: AlBe[OH/SiO$_4$]
Color: Colorless, light green or light blue; vitreous luster.
Cleavage: Highly perfect prismatic; fracture conchoidal.
Tenacity: Brittle.
Crystal Form: Monoclinic; prismatic in the longitudinal direction, usually heavily striated.
Occurrence: In druses in pegmatites.
Associated Minerals: Herderite, pericline, quartz.

Similar Minerals: Albite is softer.

2/3/4 Beryl
Hardness: 7½–8.
Density: 2.63–2.80.
Streak: White.
Chemical Formula: Al$_2$Be$_3$[Si$_6$O$_{18}$]
Color: Colorless, yellow (golden beryl), pink (morganite), red, blue (aquamarine), green (emerald); vitreous luster.
Cleavage: Sometimes discernible basal; fracture conchoidal.
Tenacity: Brittle.
Crystal Form: Hexagonal; prismatic to tabular, rarely with more faces, embedded (dull) and attached (transparent).
Occurrence: Embedded in pegmatites, attached in druses in pegmatites, in mica schists and hydrothermal calcite veins.
Associated Minerals: Feldspar, quartz, calcite.
Similar Minerals: Apatite is much softer.

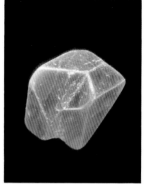

5 Spinel twin, Burma, 3x

6 Phenakite, Fichtelgebirge (Germany), 3x

7 Phenakite, Gasteiner Tal (Austria), 6x

5 Spinel

Hardness: 8.
Density: 3.6.
Streak: White.
Chemical Formula: $MgAl_2O_4$
Color: Red, violet, blue, yellow, colorless; vitreous luster.
Cleavage: Barely discernible; fracture conchoidal.
Tenacity: Brittle.
Crystal Form: Isometric; octahedrons, embedded, as irregular grains.
Occurrence: In metamorphic rocks, in marble, and in placers.
Associated Minerals: Corundum, calcite.
Similar Minerals: Corundum has a different crystal form.

6/7 Phenakite

Hardness: 8.
Density: 3.0.
Streak: White.
Chemical Formula: $Be_2[SiO_4]$
Color: Colorless, yellowish, pink, white; vitreous luster.
Cleavage: None; fracture conchoidal.
Tenacity: Brittle.
Crystal Form: Trigonal; prismatic to tabular, lenticu-lar, prisms vertically striated, embedded and attached.
Occurrence: In mica schists associated with emerald, in druses and lining fissures in pegmatites and granites.
Associated Minerals: Emerald, bertrandite, chrysoberyl, apatite.
Similar Minerals: Quartz is somewhat softer and always has horizontal banding on the prisms.

White Streak

1 Chrysoberyl, India, 2x

3 Topaz, Mursinka (Russia), 1x

2 Topaz, Schneckenstein (Vogtland, Germany), 1x

Marvelous examples of cut, polished topazes from Schneckenstein in the Vogtland are on view in Dresden, in the "Green Vault."

1 Chrysoberyl
(Alexandrite)
Hardness: 8$^{1}/_{2}$.
Density: 3.7.
Streak: White.
Chemical Formula:
Al_2BeO_4
Color: Yellow, green; vitreous luster.
Cleavage: Discernible basal; fracture conchoidal.
Tenacity: Brittle.
Crystal Form:
Orthorhombic; thick tabular, trillings resemble hexagonal bipyramids, embedded and attached.
Occurrence: In pegmatites and mica schists, embedded and attached.
Associated Minerals: Emerald, feldspar, mica.
Similar Minerals: The high hardness of chrysoberyl makes misidentification almost impossible. Topaz always has a very good cleavage.

2/3 Topaz
Hardness: 8.
Density: 3.5–3.6.
Streak: White.
Chemical Formula:
$Al_2[F_2/SiO_4]$
Color: Colorless, white, yellow, blue, green, red, pink, violet, brown; vitreous luster.
Cleavage: Perfect basal; fracture conchoidal.
Tenacity: Brittle.
Crystal Form:
Orthorhombic; short or long columnar, massive, radiated.
Occurrence: In pegmatites, pneumatolytic formations, and placers.
Associated Minerals: Cassiterite, fluorite, tourmaline, quartz.
Similar Minerals: Quartz is lighter and has no cleavage. Fluorite is much softer.

4 Ruby, Chamrray (India), 1x

6 Diamond, Kimberley (South Africa), 2x

5 Sapphire, Ratnapura (Sri Lanka), 1x

7 Diamond twin. (South Africa), 6x

4/5 Corundum
Hardness: 9.
Density: 3.9–4.1.
Streak: White.
Chemical Formula: Al_2O_3
Color: Many color varieties, including blue (sapphire), red (ruby), yellow, green, brown, violet, white, colorless; vitreous luster.
Cleavage: Poor; fracture conchoidal.
Tenacity: Brittle.
Crystal Form: Trigonal; prismatic, bipyramidal, tabular, massive.
Occurrence: In pegmatites, peridotites, amphibolites, gneisses, marbles, as inclusion in volcanic rocks, in placers.
Associated Minerals: Spinel, magnetite, calcite.
Similar Minerals: Hardness, density, and crystal form distinguish corundum from all other minerals.

6/7 Diamond
Hardness: 10.
Density: 3.52.
Streak: White.
Chemical Formula: C
Color: Colorless, white, yellow, brown, reddish, greenish, blue, gray, black; adamantine luster.
Cleavage: Perfect octahedral; fracture conchoidal.
Tenacity: Brittle.
Crystal Form: Isometric; most commonly octahedrons, more rarely cubes, radiating fibrous.
Occurrence: In kimberlites that form so-called pipes, in placers, conglomerates, and metamorphic schists.
Associated Minerals: Pyrope, olivine, phlogopite.
Similar Minerals: The great hardness distinguishes diamond from all other minerals.

211

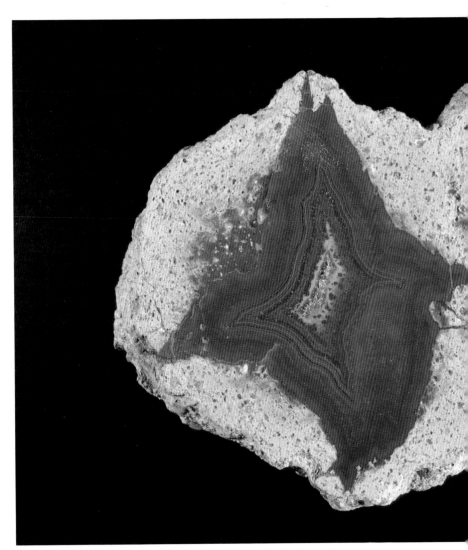

An exceptionally attractive double-chambered agate from St. Egidien in Saxony (Germany). Width, about 8 inches (20 cm). This specimen is of special interest because the agates in the two chambers have developed in entirely different ways.

Collecting
Minerals

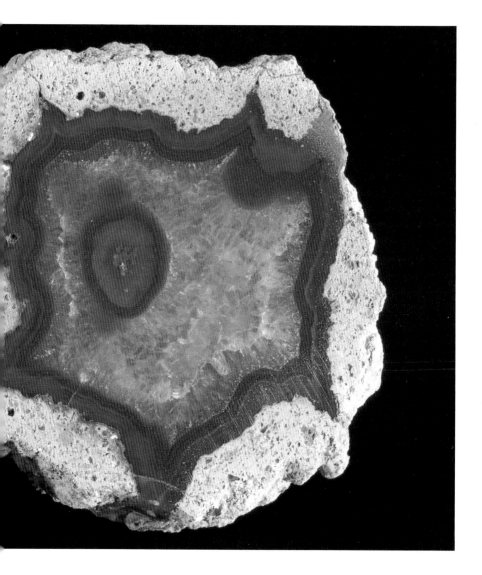

Next, you will learn where to find minerals, how to collect them in the field, how to store them, how to organize your collection, what equipment and tools you need for those purposes, and where to acquire the minerals you can't find yourself—in short, everything you need to become a successful collector of minerals, with a collection admired by all.

Finding Mineral Specimens

The first important questions for mineral collectors are, Where do I get minerals? How can I find specimens like those pictured in this book? Prospecting for minerals in the field is the most fascinating way, and also the cheapest. Minerals and crystals are to be found wherever rock is exposed. Natural causes may account for the rock's exposure in some places—for example, along the banks of rivers and streams, on rocky cliffs, or on slopes created by landslides in mountainous regions. Areas of rock, however, also may be exposed by man—say, during road construction, in quarries, and in mines—and the potential for discovery of minerals is often greatest in those places.

Where Is It All Right to Collect?

In North America and abroad, in certain regions (national parks and nature preserves), the extraction of minerals with or without tools is restricted or, in some cases, prohibited altogether. Information about such restrictions is available from the appropriate administrative authorities of the community or tourism office and state park and recreation departments or the National Park Service. In some parts of Europe, collecting minerals is possible only with a permit. There, too, local governments will provide information. In the South Tyrol (Italy), you need to apply for a collecting

permit, issued by the Association of Mineral and Fossil Collecting Societies of South Tyrol (Obstmarkt 9, I/39100 Bolzano/Italy). However, the permit is granted only to members of mineral collectors' organizations. Generally speaking, it is important to find out about any restrictions on collecting at the time you begin to plan your excursion. Because the sites often are on private property, it is essential to ask permission of the property owner or the quarry master before you enter the property and start collecting. Collecting at a quarry is best done on days when the quarriers are not at work. They will not be disturbed, nor will you. If, however, you are interested in buying specimens that have been discovered there, you need to go on a workday. In mines, on the other hand, it sometimes is possible to get permission to collect on workdays. This is handled admirably at some parks and mines, where for a modest fee collectors are allowed to search and collect all or specified minerals. If at all possible, find out in advance about such opportunities. A collecting excursion should, in any event, be planned with great care. You always need to obtain permission ahead of time, to avoid transgressing any prohibitions against collecting or trespassing on private property.

Good Planning—from Start to Finish

Before you travel to a region

about which you lack mineralogical knowledge, inform yourself about the collecting sites there; avoid unpleasant surprises and disappointments.

U.S. Sources of Information on Collection Sites

A few fairly comprehensive books on collecting localities of minerals and gems in the U.S. include *Coast to Coast Gem Atlas* and *Western Gem Hunters Atlas*, both by Rob and Cy Johnson, and published by Cy Johnson & Son, Box 288, 435 N. Roop Street, Susanville, CA 96130. These books are exactly what they seem to be: Atlases on which collection sites have been marked.

Paul Villard's *Gemstones and Minerals* (Winchester Press) offers state-by-state lists with addresses of collection sites.

Then you have the *Gem Trails* series, encompassing New Mexico, Arizona, California, and Nevada. Published by Gem Guides Book Co., 315 Cloverleaf Drive, Suite F, Baldwin Park, CA 91706. June Culp Zeitner has written *Midwest Gem, Fossil and Mineral Trails: Prairie States,* and *Midwest Gem, Fossil and Mineral Trails: Great Lake States,* also published by Gem Guides Book Co.

Every May issue of *Lapidary Journal* (Lapidary Journal Inc., 60 Chestnut Avenue, Suite 201, Devon, PA 19333-1312, phone (215) 293-1112) has a section dedicated to sources of informa-

Granite quarry near Tittling (Bavarian Forest, Germany)

tion for people planning a collection trip that includes a listing of dig-for-free areas.

Sources for Identification of Minerals

A book a bit more detailed in the description of the properties of minerals than the one you are reading is *Handbook of Rocks, Minerals and Gemstones*, by Schumann (Houghton Mifflin, 1993).

Simon & Schuster's Guide to Rocks and Minerals by Mottana, Crespi and Liborio (Simon & Schuster, NY, 1988) has more text material on mineral properties and crystal chemistry.

Photo: Quarries make especially interesting places to find minerals, because new material is constantly coming to light. Before visiting such a locality, however, you always have to ask the owner's permission.

Collecting Minerals

Various geological hammers

Journals and E-Mail

Three important U.S. journals are *Lapidary Journal* (see address above), *Rock and Gem* magazine (4880 Market Street, Ventura, CA 93003, phone (805) 644-3824), and *Mineralogical Record* (7413 N. Mowry Place, Tucson, AZ 85741).

There are two e-mail lists accessible via Internet, offering the opportunity to communicate with other collectors who can provide suggestions and up-to-date information. One of these is Rocks-and-fossils @Athena.MIT.EDU, and the other is Rockhounds@info-dyne.com.

Maps

Now you have gathered enough information about the site and its minerals. In order to find it—often such a locality may be an old dump some-where in the woods—you need good maps and charts. If the site in question is not a large mine or a good-sized quarry, road maps will not be adequate. Trail maps with a scale of 1:100,000 are suitable for this purpose, but 1:50,000 is better, as are ordnance survey maps on a scale of 1:25,000. Plot the exact route on the map ahead of time. In addition, once you are in the vicinity you can contact a collector who lives near the site (addresses are available, for example, in the membership list of a local mineralogical society). Alternatively, you can ask the author of a relevant magazine article to give you directions.

Always use some caution in evaluating information on the potential for discovery. Localities that a collector of

Photo: Geological hammers with points and edges are available in a variety of models. For collecting minerals in the field, hammers with an edge can be employed for a wider range of purposes.

large specimens believes to be exhausted may prove to be a bounty for an attentive collector of micromount material, which requires a microscope for proper observation. For a collector of beautifully crystallized specimens, a site with very rare but relatively massive minerals may have been completely unproductive. A collector who believes he or she has not found a single usable mineral on a dump may simply have been digging in the wrong place. In

Search and Discovery

quarries that are still in operation, conditions often change quite rapidly. Someone who found nothing at all the previous month might find wonderful specimens today in almost the same spot.

Equipment

If your efforts at field collecting are to succeed, you also need the proper equipment. The following implements are necessary:

- A standard hammer (weighing about 17 ounces [500 g]) for shattering small specimens and for more delicate chisel work (a hammer with a steel handle is preferable).
- A standard mason's hammer for heavier work.
- Various chisels (flat chisels and pointed chisels), at least one large one for heavy jobs and one small one for finer work.
- For searching on old dumps, a collapsible shovel and a hammer with an edge as wide as possible.
- Protective goggles, to keep your eyes from being injured by flying chips and slivers when you are working with a hammer and chisel.
- Packing materials, so that you can bring home safely the specimens you've found: newspapers for less delicate specimens, soft paper or expanded plastics for fragile ones, small bags or tiny boxes for little ones.
- Transport equipment: If you drive right to the site, a sturdy picnic basket is better suited to hold your discoveries than a backpack, although the latter, of course, is indispensable if much hiking is involved.

Behavior at the Site

Once at the site, it is best to first gather information at the places where other people have hammered or dug before you. Often collectors will have piled up in one spot any specimens they were unable to use. There you'll be able to see right away what there is to be found and what you have to watch for. Among the discarded specimens you also may find something you can use yourself.

One last, urgent request: Leave the site as you found it. In quarries, too, a certain order prevails. It is irresponsible for collectors to leave behind deep holes and blocks that have tumbled down.

Buying Minerals

If you would like to make your collection complete, on occasion you will have to buy minerals that you can't find yourself.

In recent years a large number of mail-order dealers and rock shops have gone into business because of the constantly rising demand. Not all of these enterprises, however, are managed with the proper expertise. Because the uniqueness of each and every specimen makes fixed prices for minerals an impossibility, pricing is entirely in the hands of the individual merchants. For this reason, there may be extremely large differences in the prices of similar specimens.

In the last few years the number of mineral shows also has increased markedly. At these shows collectors have an opportunity to see a large array of minerals of all kinds, compare prices, and buy specimens. However, because the cost of renting a stand at the large shows is frequently high, the mineral specimens for sale there may often not be cheaper than in a store, but be more costly.

Trading Minerals

The third possible way to acquire minerals is through exchange. Mineralogical societies—local, statewide, and national—hold monthly meetings for their members at which talks are presented and there is an opportunity to trade specimens and exchange information. Some associations organize international trading days—like those held annually in Hannover and in Kempen on the Lower Rhine—with lectures and excursions.

You can also trade specimens by mail. First, lists of specimens wanted and offered are sent. If the two correspondents agree on what they want and on the procedures, the minerals are shipped. They will not become your property, however, until your trading partner has agreed to the deal.

Good packaging is extremely important when you ship specimens.

Organizing a Mineral Collection

At the beginning, mineral lovers probably will collect every obtainable specimen. After a relatively short time the number of minerals will have grown so large that the collector will have to think about collecting with a certain purpose in mind and about limiting the size of the collection.

The Systematic Collection

A systematic collection is the most comprehensive, because it is intended to include, insofar as possible, all known minerals. Not an easy task: Far more than 3,000 minerals are known today, and about 30 new ones are identified each year!

Even in museums and institutions of mineralogy there exists no complete systematic collection. A collection containing over 1,000 different minerals is to be considered a very good one. For a beginner, 300 to 500 mineral species would be remarkable.

An ambitious systematic collection, moreover, should document the major sites, crystal forms, types of habit, and parageneses of each mineral. This kind of collection is more or less a bottomless pit: You can indeed strive for completeness, but you will never attain it. That is, however, also one of the special charms of a systematic collection: You can work on it all your life, and

you still will come across new specimens to add.

The Specialized Collection

Completeness is more easily achieved if you start specialized collections, that is, collections that deal with only a part of the large domain of minerals. Here there are no limits to your fantasy. Particularly rewarding areas for specialized collectors are, for example, the copper oxidation minerals, the minerals of the zeolite group, or phosphate minerals. Other areas might be twins or various developments of a single mineral, such as quartz.

The Regional Collection

Another scientifically interesting type of specialized collection is the localized collection. It contains the minerals from a single collecting site or region, but if at all possible it should be complete, with all developments and parageneses. Here it is helpful to set up a good systematic collection in addition, for comparison. In most cases, advanced collectors have a systematic collection as well as several regional and specialized collections.

Size of the Specimens

As the extent of the mineral collection grows, the question of specimen size arises. If the

collection is to be attractive, the specimens need to be approximately equal in size. Almost no one can afford—in terms of both financial expenditures and space requirements—to collect large specimens measuring over 6×8 inches (15×20 cm). That is a task for a museum or a mineralogical institution—and such splendid specimens often are known as museum specimens precisely for that reason. Specimens ranging from 2×3 inches (5×7 cm) to $3^1/_2 \times 4^3/_4$ inches (9×12 cm) are a good compromise. Their size means that they are not overly expensive, and they do not take up too much room.

Micromounts

In recent years a new way of collecting minerals has developed in the United States: The collecting of micromounts, small specimens no bigger than $^3/_4 \times ^3/_4$ inch (2×2 cm) that require magnification to observe properly. The advantage of these tiny specimens is that they take up little room and are much cheaper than larger materials. For collectors who observe their specimens for the first time through a stereomicroscope, a world of unsuspected beauty is revealed. The acquisition of a stereomicroscope does indeed entail a relatively large one-time expenditure, but it is quickly offset by the reduced

From Micromount to Museum Specimen

Small boxes of minerals in a collector's cabinet

cost of the minerals. Before purchasing such an expensive piece of equipment (about $200 and up), you should consult friends who are collectors and try out the various models. A stereomicroscope is virtually indispensable at present for all advanced collectors (not only for micromount collectors), invaluable for use in identifying the minerals they have found.

Storing Mineral Specimens

It is best to keep mineral specimens in small plastic boxes, available in mineral shops. Little cardboard boxes are only slightly cheaper, but less sturdy. If possible, buy only boxes that allow you to use the available space without any waste. The more different sizes you use, the more difficult that becomes. For this reason, confine yourself to

about two or three box sizes. First put a label in the box giving the name, number, and site of the mineral. For protection, place a small piece of transparent plastic over the label; then put the mineral on the plastic. It is essential to affix the specimen's identification number firmly to the mineral, to rule out mix-ups when several specimens are taken out at once. Micromounts, again, are a special case. They need to be glued in tiny boxes with adhesive. Then the collection will look much neater and be easier to handle. In this case the labels also need to be glued to the little boxes. No additional marking of the mineral is necessary, because the adhesive firmly bonds the specimen to the little box bearing the label.

Some collectors have switched to storing larger specimens in boxes also, be-

cause they are better protected from dust there. Larger boxes, however, are so costly that this type of storage is not yet widespread.

Naturally, a special custom-made storage cabinet for minerals is the best place to keep all the boxes, but it is also the most expensive. For this reason, standard cabinets usually have to serve as substitutes. Office cabinets with shallow drawers for filing forms are very practical. The drawers ought not to be overly large, so that when full they can still be pulled out easily.

The Collector's Card Index
Although your collection may be nicely stowed away in

Collecting Minerals

cabinets, it can happen that you find a certain specimen only after a long search. Usually, too, there is not nearly enough room on the label in the little box to hold all the necessary information. Both these problems can be solved by an index card. There are two useful possibilities:

1. For each mineral, fill out a separate index card. A 3 × 5-inch card is best, as it saves space. The following information should appear on the card:

- identification number of the mineral
- name
- chemical formula
- color
- form and habit
- collection site (without this information the mineral is practically worthless for your collection)
- date found
- finder
- origin of the mineral (for example, found by you, exchanged, or purchased)
- associated minerals
- special treatment of the specimen (for example, acidified with HCl)
- location in your collection

It is debatable whether it is necessary to list additional properties of the mineral, such as the hardness, density, and streak. It also depends on your diligence, on whether you want to enter "Hardness 3" over and over for 20 calcites.

A more practical solution may be to make out a card for each mineral, enumerating all the properties, and place it in front of the other cards for the given mineral in your catalog.

To make a mineral easy to find, arrange the cards according to the mineral identification numbers.

Some collectors simply number their specimens sequentially. This method has drawbacks, however: First,

such a number is merely a group of digits and tells you nothing about the mineral; second, you also have to attach a list in which all the numbers for a given mineral are entered, because someday you might want to find all the quartzes—but with this method of numbering, their cards would be scattered throughout the entire card index.

A better way is to assign the specimen a number in accordance with the classification system used for minerals in crystal chemistry (see page 10). The phosphates, for example, all have Roman numeral VII; A means anhydrous with no foreign anions; and 1 refers to the berlinite-beryllonite-hurlbutite group. The next number, then, signifies the individual mineral in the group; in this way the mineral is labeled unambiguously. Berlinite, for example,

Photo: The author's collection. Minerals can be safely stored in cabinets, with drawers that are not too large or too deep for easy access.

Labels and Card Index

has the number VII/A.1-1. The individual specimens of this same mineral species are numbered quite normally from 1 on, consecutively. Berlinite specimen number 1, then, has the identification number VII/A.1-1.1.

The advantage of this method is that the cards for all the specimens of a mineral species are arranged one after another in the index, and you can lay your hands on them immediately.

Preprinted index cards are now available in many shops that sell mineral specimens.

It is best to store the cards in small plastic file-card boxes, like those available in office supply stores.

2. For the second method of cataloging, you need a loose-leaf notebook. For each mineral species, set up a file page that contains all the invariable properties. On the same page, enter the individual specimens in a table that has columns for

all the important information (as listed before in 1). The advantage of this method is that it is easy to use because all the specimens of the same mineral species are cataloged on a single page.

In this age of computers, of course, there are many collectors who use their PCs to manage their collections. Programs for this purpose, tailored to the needs of mineral collectors, are available in software stores. This method naturally offers great advantages, because with the proper programs all the desired data can be searched for and called up at the touch of a key. However, a customized system can cost a thousand dollars or more, and the general-data commercial programs are not inexpensive either. If you know something about computers, however, you can put together a suitable program yourself, or adapt a less expensive general-purpose database to suit your own

requirements. Computers also are ideal for producing up-to-date lists of wanted minerals and/or minerals available for exchange.

Rock Collecting

What are rocks? Rocks are bodies of natural origin that are composed of many minerals of the same or different species and are measured in terms ranging from feet to miles. A rock may be so fine-grained that the individual mineral grains can be discerned only under a microscope, but it also may be so coarse-grained that individual bodies measure several yards across. The components of rocks need not, as in the case of granite and marble, be firmly cemented together. As with sand or gravel, rocks also may be made up of many small, loose parts that can be moved toward each other. The outer shape of a rock is always determined by its environment and is only conditionally characteristic of its species. A rock can constitute a mountain, fill in a crack in the surrounding strata, be hammered into pieces, or be decomposed into grains by weathering—it always remains a rock, whatever its external configuration. A rock also may consist of fragments of other rocks. That is the case with gravel and the conglomerates created from it, as well as the breccias.

The Origin of Rocks

According to their mode of formation, rocks are divided into three great successions:
1. The igneous succession includes all rocks that were formed from molten masses. If the magma hardened at great depth in the earth, the resulting rocks are known as plutonic rocks, such as granite, diorite, and syenite. If it solidified at the earth's surface, the rocks are known as extrusive or volcanic rocks, such as basalt, andesite, and rhyolite.
2. The sedimentary succession includes rocks that were formed by weathering, transportation, and deposition (sedimentation). Examples are sand, sandstone, and limestone. Their formation was caused by both physical and chemical processes.
3. The metamorphic succession includes rocks that were created from other rocks by changes in pressure, temperature, or both. Examples are mica schist, gneiss, and eclogite.
a. We use the term contact metamorphism when high temperatures produced by the intrusions of magma alone, act to alter rock that has already solidified.
b. Regional metamorphism occurs when rock masses are transported to greater depths, and in this process the temperature and the pressure rise simultaneously.
c. In dynamic (dislocation) metamorphism, masses of rock are buried at considerable depths so quickly that only the increase in pressure can act on the rock.

Locating Specimens

The entire terrestrial globe consists of rocks. For this reason, they can be collected wherever the uppermost layer of soil has been carried away or was never present at all. As in the case of minerals, collectors will find especially favorable conditions in quarries. There the rock is bare and still fresh, unaltered by weathering. Additional places of discovery are cliffs and slopes with heaps of coarse debris at the foot (scree, talus), but rocks also can be found in fields where the soil has been freshly turned over.

Geological guidebooks, for example, provide information on especially interesting exposures where rock can be seen in place.

The specimens collected should display all the major features of a rock. If the rock is extremely fine-grained, a relatively small piece will adequately reveal the structure and all the constituents. On the other hand, you will have to place a much larger piece of a coarse-grained type, say, granite, in your collection to show all the features. If the feldspars in this rock are as large as 4 inches (10 cm), a specimen measuring 4×2 inches (10×5 cm) can never represent the entire rock. As a rule, rectangular specimens of convenient size—about $3^1/_2 \times 4^3/_4$ inches (9×12 cm)—are cut.

The Rock Collection

Gneiss, a metamorphic rock from Herkjinn in the province of Österdalen (Norway)

Rocks should be stored and classified in the same way as minerals. A good rock collection ought to contain, if possible, all the developmental forms of a species of rock. That is, not just one granite, but the most diverse types of this rock—for example, biotite granite, two-mica granite, crystal granite, fine-grained granite, coarse-grained granite, porphyritic granite, or granite from a variety of locations.

Of special interest—and less demanding in terms of space—are collections that provide an inventory of the rocks in a certain region or of a certain geological unit.

Photo: The gneiss shown above is an extremely inhomogeneous conglomerate gneiss, in which the former rock fragments, now altered through metamorphism, are still easily discernible. Size of the specimen is about 12 inches (30 cm). Obviously, a much smaller specimen could not provide a comprehensive view of the gneiss' composition because of the coarse structure of the rock.

Short Glossary of Mineralogical Terms

Aggregate: Intergrowth of several crystals. Aggregates may be globular, fibrous, reniform, or radiating fibrous.

Alpha rays: Helium atoms with a double positive charge (He^{+2}).

Alpine cavities (vugs): Hollows in silicate rock. They may be partially or entirely filled with mineral formations. (See CAVITIES.)

Alpine cavity

Alteration pseudomorph: One mineral is replaced by another, chemically unrelated one, while the crystal form is preserved.

Amorphous: Not crystalline; minerals that possess no crystal structure.

Amphiboles: Group of silicates with a typical CLEAVAGE ANGLE of about 120°.

Anisotropic: Applied to crystals displaying unequal physical properties in different directions. For example, the hardness of disthene, which is 4 to $4^{1}/_{2}$ lengthwise and 6 to 7 crosswise.

Arid: Dry, desertlike.

Associated minerals: Minerals that appear with the mineral being described in a common paragenesis.

Asterism: Property of various crystals that reflect incident light in the shape of a star.

Atom: Smallest particle of an element; no longer divisible by chemical agents.

Attached crystals: Crystals that project into empty cavities (see EMBEDDED CRYSTALS).

Axis of symmetry (rotation axis): Imaginary axis through the midpoint of a crystal, about which a crystal can be turned at a certain angle (angle of rotation) so that it reaches a position identical to its original one. Depending on how often you have to rotate the crystal to bring it back to the initial position, the axis is one of twofold, threefold, fourfold, or sixfold symmetry.

Base (basal pinacoid): Parallel pair of faces perpendicular to the c axis. A base is present in tetragonal, hexagonal, trigonal, and orthorhombic CRYSTAL SYSTEMS. The base is an open form and can appear only in combination with other forms, for example, with prisms, which it closes like a "cap."

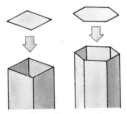

A basal face "closes" a prism.

Bean (pisolitic) iron ore: Globular aggregates consisting of limonite that occur in karst cavities as weathering formations. Bean iron ore was mined as iron ore in previous times.

Beta rays: Electron rays.

Bipyramid (dipyramid): Crystal form symmetrical about a plane dividing it into two pyramids.

Birefringence (double refraction): A ray of light traveling through a crystal is split into two rays that are

Short Glossary of Mineralogical Terms

polarized perpendicular to each other. The ordinary or primary ray, upon entry at a right angle, passes through the crystal in a straight line, while the secondary ray is diffracted. The refractive indices for the two rays are different.

Brilliant cut: A type of cut used for gems.

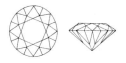

Brilliant cut, seen from above (left) and from the side (right).

Brittle: Said of a mineral if its particles jump away when it is penetrated by a sharp object (see NONBRITTLE).

Cabochon cut: In this type of cut, rounded bodies are cut with a smooth basal surface.

Carbonates: Compounds of elements with the CO_3^{-2} group.

Caves: Relatively large cavities in rock, especially in carbonate and sulfate rocks.

Cavities: Hollow areas that develop in rock because of some form of stress.

Cavity minerals: Minerals that are created when hot water from cavities in the rock circulates, dissolves out substances from the rock, and redeposits them on the cavity

wall in the form of well-crystallized minerals.

Cementation zone: Area of the groundwater table in which certain elements are concentrated.

Cleavage angle: Angle at which the cleavage surfaces of a mineral intersect.

Compound: Chemical substance—halite or rock salt (NaCl), for example—made up of several kinds of atoms.

Concretion: Knobby or rounded mineral concentrations in SEDIMENTARY ROCKS that are completely enclosed by the surrounding rock.

Constituents: Mineral species of which a rock is made up. Primary constituents form the major portion of a rock and account for large percentages of the total mass. Secondary constituents each make up 1 percent or less of the specimen.

Contact metamorphism: Change of a rock due to the effect of high temperatures during contact with a lava flow, magma sloping, or igneous intrusion.

Contact metasomatic formations: When solutions or vapors that come from the MAGMA alter the surrounding rock at the place of contact between the magma and the surrounding rock.

Contact rock: Rock created through the action of high temperatures.

Crystal classes: On the basis of their symmetry, crystals are divided into 32 crystal classes.

Crystallization: Point in time at which a substance forms crystals.

Crystallography: The study of crystals.

Crystal system: All the crystals that are related to the same axis of symmetry belong to a crystal system; there are seven such systems.

Dendrites: Skeletal crystals that develop from supersaturated solutions, often in narrow cracks. Frequently they resemble plants or trees. Manganese oxides, silver, copper, and gold are particularly apt to form dendrites.

Dendrites (skeletal crystals) on a limestone slab.

Deposit: Natural accumulation of minerals at a certain site on Earth.

Diamagnetism: Property of substances that contain no magnetism.

Short Glossary of Mineralogical Terms

Dome: Open crystallographic form consisting of two nonparallel faces that meet to form a roof shape.

Double spar (Iceland spar, Iceland crystal): Clear calcite that because of its strong double refraction doubles the image of lines placed under it.

Doubly terminated crystals: Crystals that have grown freely and are developed on all sides.

Attached crystals (left, see glossary) and free-growing crystals (right, see glossary), so-called doubly terminated crystals.

Dripstones: Conelike structures that grow upward (stalagmites) or downward (stalactites).

Druses: Roundish cavities in rock, in which crystals grow. Some also use it to describe the crusts of crystals filling the cavity.

Ductile: Capable of being stretched, molded, or shaped.

Element: Chemical substance that is made up of only a single type of atom—for example, iron, lead, or gold.

Embedded crystals: Crystals that are surrounded by rock on all sides.

Endogenous: Generated in the bowels of the earth by forces such as volcanism or earthquakes.

Epitaxy: Crystallographically oriented overgrowth of one mineral species on another. On an already existing crystal face of one partner (the "host") form nuclei of the other partner (the "guest"). These oriented nuclei subsequently grow into visible crystals.

Epizone: In regional metamorphism, the depth level nearest to the surface. It extends to a depth of about 3 3/4 to 4 1/3 miles (6–7 km).

Extrusive (igneous) rocks: Rocks that solidify at the surface of the earth.

Faceted gems: Gems that are cut so that they are completely bounded by planar surfaces.

Ferromagnetism: Property of materials that are magnetic even in the absence of an external magnetic field.

Fibrous or layered sphalerite: Reniform, crusty, alternate banding of sphalerite with marcasite and wurtzite.

Flotation: Dressing of ores by means of liquids. The ore is powdered, suspended, and diluted with reagents that cause it to float on the top when air is injected; undesirable admixtures sink to the bottom.

Fluorescence: Property of certain minerals that display luminescence (fluoresce) when illuminated with UV light. The color of fluorescence can be an identifying property for a certain mineral.

Fluvial: Deposits from rivers.

Form: The set of all the faces appearing on a crystal; independent of the general appearance of the crystal.

Fracture: Shape of the fracture surface (plane)—for example, conchoidal, uneven, hackly. Not to be confused with cleavage. A cleavage surface is not a fracture surface. In minerals with perfect cleavage there often are no true fracture surfaces.

Fumaroles: Spots in or near active volcanoes where gases are expelled.

Gamma rays: Short-wave electromagnetic waves.

Gangue minerals: Minerals that are associated with ore minerals in veins of ore—for example, calcite, barite, fluorite, quartz, and siderite.

Gemstones (precious stones): Minerals that are noted for their hardness, high optical refraction, and rarity and are used for ornamentation—for example, diamond, ruby, sapphire, and emerald.

Short Glossary of Mineralogical Terms

Geode: Roundish cavity in volcanic rock lined with crystals.

Grain boundary: Boundary between two intergrown mineral grains. Because the mechanical strength is lowest at that place, WEATHERING usually begins there.

Graphic granite: Special type of intergrowth of quartz and feldspar in which structures resembling script result.

Greenstone: Metamorphic rock of the epizone that contains epidote, chlorite, and other green minerals.

Greisen: Name given to granite altered by PNEUMATOLYSIS.

Habit: Characteristic appearance of a crystal.

Halides: Compounds of elements with the halogens fluorine, chlorine, bromine, and iodine.

HCl test: The mineral to be tested is moistened with a drop of hydrochloric acid. Exercise caution when using acids; they can produce serious burns on your skin! Rinse with water immediately.

Highly volatile: Said of substances that readily pass into the gaseous phase. They become increasingly concentrated during the crystallization

of MAGMA and result in PEG-MATITE and PNEUMATOLYTIC FORMATIONS.

Hydrostatic balance: Balance especially for measuring density.

Hydrothermal minerals: Minerals that have formed from solutions.

Hydrothermal veins: Fractures in rocks lined by minerals formed from solutions.

Hygroscopic: Attracting water.

Idiomorphic crystals: Crystals that arose in their own fully developed crystal form; their growth was unaffected by outside influences.

Igneous rocks: Rocks that are formed from magma.

Igneous succession: Classification for minerals and rocks that were formed from a molten mass, or whose development was caused by the presence of a magma.

Impregnation: Lining of minute cavities within a rock by a mineral of later origin.

Inclusions: Substances that are enclosed within a mineral as it forms—for example, other minerals, gas bubbles, and liquids.

Ion: Electrically charged atom or group of atoms.

Iron hat: Old miner's term for the OXIDATION ZONE.

Isometric crystals: Crystals that cover roughly the same area in all three dimensions.

Isotropization: Destruction of the crystal lattice by intense radioactive bombardment.

Kaolinite: Conglomerate of various clay minerals.

Lava: Molten rock that issues at Earth's surface.

Luster: As perceived by the eye, the overall impression of refraction and reflection of incident light by a mineral.

Magma: Molten rock material in the bowels of the earth.

Massive: Minerals that are bounded not by crystal faces, but only by irregular fracture surfaces or cleavage surfaces.

Melting point: Temperature at which the atom lattice disintegrates and the building blocks of the lattice become free to move. The temperature at which a solid becomes a liquid.

Metamict minerals: Minerals whose crystal lattice was

Short Glossary of Mineralogical Terms

destroyed by radioactive bombardment. Conchoidal fracture and pitchy luster are characteristic of metamict minerals. The external crystal form, however, is retained.

Metamorphic succession: Classification for minerals and rocks that were created from others by alteration, during changes in pressure or temperature, or both.

Metamorphism: Alteration of rocks by the action of pressure or temperature, or both.

Metasomatism: Alteration of a rock by addition or exchange of components.

Metastable: Said of minerals that exist outside their normal field of stability.

Meteorite: Solid body that comes from outer space and penetrates Earth's atmosphere.

Miaroles: Small cavities in granitic rocks created by highly volatile components.

Micromount: SPECIMEN no more than $^3/_4 \times {}^3/_4$ inch (2×2 cm) in size.

Miller indices: Group of three digits used to designate crystal faces. They indicate the inclination of a given face with respect to the axes of the systems of coordinates.

Minerals: Naturally occurring bodies with uniform composition.

Mixed crystal (solid solution): Crystals that contain two or more compounds in variable proportions.

Mohs hardness scale: Sequence of 10 minerals, each of which will scratch the preceding one.

Monochromatic: Said of minerals that are self-colored or whose color is characteristic and remains approximately the same even at different sites.

Moonstone: White plagioclase that has a white glimmer.

Mountain leather: Matlike, fibrous, leathery masses of chrysotile and other minerals.

Multicolored: Minerals that vary in color from one region to another. Different colors may appear even at the same site, indeed even in the same specimen.

Native: Metals that appear in elemental form in natural deposits.

Nitrates: Compounds of elements with the NO_3^- group.

Nonbrittle: A mineral is not brittle if particles are left on

the edge of the furrow when the substance is penetrated by a hard object (see BRITTLE).

Occurrence: Preferential appearance of a given mineral in certain rocks or deposits.

Opaque: Not transparent or translucent.

Ore: Miner's term for a mineral or mineral conglomerate that contains an element in sufficient quantity to permit its extraction at a profit.

Ore deposits: Deposits that contain an ore in sufficient quantity to make its recovery and extraction worthwhile.

Ore minerals: Minerals that are noted for their high specific gravity and/or metallic to semimetallic LUSTER.

Orogenesis: Complex of phenomena that lead to the formation of a mountain range.

Orthoclase: A feldspar.

Oxidation minerals: Minerals of the OXIDATION ZONE that were formed from the existing ore minerals.

Oxidation zone: Area of a deposit that is exposed to the influence of weathering through the admission of water, atmospheric oxygen, and CO_2.

Short Glossary of Mineralogical Terms

Oxides: Compounds of elements with oxygen.

Paragenesis: Orderly occurrence of certain minerals during the formation of rocks and deposits.

Paramorphism: Process by which a mineral species formed at high temperatures converts, if the temperature falls, to an aggregate of crystals of the modification that is stable at the new temperature. The external crystal form is not modified.

Pegmatite: Coarse-grained rock consisting primarily of potassium feldspar and quartz.

Penetration twin: TWIN in which the two crystals are intergrown in a cruciform arrangement.

Petrography: Branch of mineralogy that deals with rocks—their structure and mineral constituents.

Phantoms: Inclusions deposited in layers so as to simulate ZONING.

Phenocryst: Crystal that is set in a finer-grained ground mass.

Phosphates: Compounds of elements with the PO_4^{-3} group.

Phosphorescence: Photoluminescence of minerals that continues after excitation by UV light has ceased.

Pipes: Tubular ascending structures in volcanic rocks.

Placers: Concentrations of resistant, usually relatively heavy minerals resulting from the transport of the other rock components; depending on the place and mechanism of concentration, we distinguish between river, beach, marine, and surf placers.

Plane of symmetry: Plane through which a crystal can be divided into two like parts, each the mirror image of the other.

Pleochroism: Property of certain crystals that disperse light in several directions, resulting in a variety of colors.

Plutonic rock (pluton): Rock that solidified deep underground.

Plutonic rock   Sediment

Metamorphic rock

From a plutonic rock and a sediment, each typical in its makeup, the same metamorphic rock can result, provided the overall chemism is identical.

Pneumatolysis: Action of the gases of a magma on the surrounding rocks and on the solidifying molten mass itself.

Pneumatolytic formations: Created from the gaseous phase.

Primary minerals: Minerals that were formed first.

Prospecting: Searching or exploring for useful mineral resources.

Pseudomorph: One mineral with the crystal form of another mineral.

Pure substance: Chemical substance that contains no elements other than those to which it is entitled according to an ideal formula, in the prescribed proportions.

Pyroxenes: Group of SILICATES that are characterized by a cleavage angle of 90°.

Quartz porphyry: Traditional German name for rhyolite extrusions that are old in geological terms. Also an acid rock with over 65 percent silica and 10 percent quartz.

Radioactive: Emitting alpha, beta, or gamma rays.

Rare earths: Group of elements that are chemically very similar and almost always appear together.

Refraction of light: Occurs when a ray of light enters a different medium and is deflected.

Short Glossary of Mineralogical Terms

Refractive index _n_: Number that tells how much a substance will refract light.

Regional metamorphism: Sinking of a section of rock into greater depths, which causes the pressure and temperature to rise.

Replacement: Process whereby one mineral takes the place of another.

Retrograde metamorphism: Metamorphism that runs its course at diminishing temperatures and pressures. High-pressure and high-temperature minerals are changed into minerals that are stable at lower temperatures and pressures.

Rich ore zone: Concentration of certain elements in the area of the groundwater table.

Rock: Extensive geologic body composed of minerals.

Salts: Water-soluble halogen compounds that form their own deposits, created by the evaporation of sea water.

Sclerometer: Device for quantitative determination of hardness.

Secondary minerals: Minerals that are formed by alteration at the expense of preexisting minerals (primary minerals).

Sedimentary rock: More or less fine-grained weathering residue which, for example, has been transported by water or wind and later redeposited. Dissolved substances are precipitated out again and also form sedimentary rocks.

Sedimentary succession: Classification for minerals and rocks that were created by chemical or physical weathering and by sedimentation.

Selvage (salband): Area bordering a vein.

Silicates: Minerals that contain silicon and oxygen, in addition to other elements.

Skarn: Contact rock of igneous silicate masses with limestone.

Soil: Uppermost residual layer of the Earth's surface, heavily permeated with plant substances.

Solfataras: Vents or areas that give off gases from inactive volcanoes.

Specimen: Intergrowth of several crystals of the same species or of several mineral species. Normally specimens are collected in sizes ranging from 2×3 inches (5×7 cm) to $3\frac{1}{2} \times 4\frac{3}{4}$ inches (9×12 cm).

Specimen of convenient size: Rock sample that has been trimmed to approximately $3\frac{1}{2} \times 4\frac{3}{4}$ inches (9×12 cm) for inclusion in a rock collection.

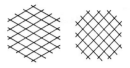

Different cleavage angles: right, in pyroxene, about 90°; left, in amphibolene, about 120°.

Spherulites: Globular or radiated aggregates that have developed outward from a center, radiating in all directions within the available space.

Stalactites: Conelike structures that grow in a downward direction, also called dripstones.

Stalagmites: Conelike structures that grow in an upward direction, also called dripstones.

Stratification: Deposition in layers of SEDIMENTARY ROCKS in which differences in the homogeneity of the particles are present. A rock that consists of completely identical particles cannot be stratified.

Streak plate: Unglazed white porcelain plate that is used to determine the color of a mineral's streak.

Structure: Regular arrangement of the atoms in a crystal.

Short Glossary of Mineralogical Terms

Subvolcanic formations: Formations that developed directly below a volcano, inside Earth's crust.

Successions: Developmental sequences for minerals and rocks.

Sulfates: Compounds of elements with the SO_4^{-2} group.

Sulfides: Compounds of elements with sulfur.

Syngenetic: Having originated at the same time as the surroundings.

Systematic collection: Collection that includes, if possible, all known minerals.

Systems of axes: Crystallographic reference systems that are used to depict the faces of a crystal.

Tarnish colors: Colors that are created on the surface of certain minerals by the formation of thin films of oxidation.

Tectonics: Science of the structure of Earth's crust.

Tenacity: Toughness, cohesiveness; way in which a substance reacts when penetrated by a sharp, harder substance (see NONBRITTLE and BRITTLE).

Transparent: Said of a crystal if the light is not weakened or is only slightly weakened on its path through it. Depending on the extent to which the light intensity is diminished, the crystal may be translucent or opaque. There are no crystals that admit no kind of light at all. For example, many ores that in normal light appear completely opaque are transparent in the infrared region. Transparency also depends on the density of the layer being illuminated. Even an opaque mineral can be transparent in thin slivers. In a mineral that is by nature transparent, opacity may be caused by inclusions.

Trillings: Regular intergrowths of three crystals of the same mineral species.

Trunk: Individual parts of a vein.

Twins: Crystals of the same species that are intergrown in a regular association.

Varieties: Variant forms of a mineral that are distinguished by a particular developmental form (color, habit).

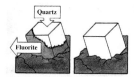

Fluorite, while retaining its crystal form, is replaced by quartz.

Vein: Filling in of a crack in the rock with minerals that are newer than the rock. The rock that has been penetrated is called the surrounding rock, and the boundary with the vein is known as the SELVAGE.

Venting: Escape of gases from the interior of the earth.

Volcanic efflorescences: Minerals created from volcanic gases.

Volcanic rocks: Rocks that solidify at Earth's surface.

Volcanic slags: Porous pyroclastic rocks that have been baked together.

Weathering: Disintegration of a mineral or rock as a result of chemical, physical, or biological factors.

Xenomorphic crystals: Crystals that do not display their characteristic crystal form, but are bounded by irregular surfaces.

Zeolites: Tectosilicates that in a solution are capable of exchanging the ions incorporated in their structure for ions of the solution without destroying the structure; they are used, for example, in softening water.

Zoning: Certain deviation from the ideal crystal caused by a difference—in terms of layers or bands—in its chemical structure.

Index

The numbers in **bold** type refer to photographs

Index

Index

Index

Index

Copyright, Credits, Acknowledgments

All the photos used in this nature guide come from the archives of the German mineralogy journal *Lapis*.

The Photographers:
Rassenberg: 53 left, 146 left. Rewitzer: 71 top left, 128 bottom right, 160 top left, 167 top left. Weiss: 25, 31, 52 bottom right, 54 top right, 57, 58 top, 62 left, 63 bottom left, 65, 67, 70 left, 75 top right, 86, 89 left, 90 left, 92 right, 93 left, 94 right, 96 bottom right, 97 right, 100 top right, bottom, 101 top left, 103 top right, 106 right, 107 right, 108 bottom right, 109 top right, 116 top, 118 top right, 119 top right, 129 right, 133 top, 135 top left, top right, 138 top left, 140, 143 left, top right, 157 top left, 170 top left, top right, 182 left, 183 right, 188 top right, bottom right, bottom left, 190 left, top right, 191 top left, 196 left, 206 bottom right, 212, 216. Hochleitner: all other photos.

Acknowledgments
Numerous institutions and private collectors allowed specimens to be photographed for inclusion in this nature guide. The author wishes to express his gratitude to the following museums and collectors, as well as to others, too numerous to be listed here: State Mineralogical Collection, Munich; Chair of Applied Mineralogy, Technical University of Munich; Petrography Institute, University of Munich; Marburg Mineralogical Museum; Mining Academy of Freiberg/Saxony; Gerhard Schweisfurth; Christian Weise; Dr. Gunther Grundmann; Andreas Weerth; Werner Leonhard; Bernd Lahl.

The U.S. editor gratefully acknowledges the help provided by Mr. Clint Hatchett, technical advisor for the English translation, and Ms. Suzanne Wade, assistant editor at *Lapidary Journal*.

The Author
Dr. Rupert Hochleitner has a degree in mineralogy. His special fields of interest are systematic mineralogy and mineral sites. He teaches in the Adult Education Program in Munich, Germany. Dr. Hochleitner is editor in chief of the German mineralogy journal *LAPIS* and the author of successful books on identifying minerals and guides to mineral sites.

Basic Books
When essential data have to be found fast, two pocket-sized *Mini Fact Finders* from Barron's provide invaluable help:
Rupert Hochleitner: *Gemstones*, 1990.
Rupert Hochleitner: *Minerals*, 1990.

Library of Congress Cataloging-in-Publication Data

Hochleitner, Rupert.
　　[Mineralien. English]
　　Minerals : identifying, classifying, and collecting them / Rupert Hochleitner ; [translated from the German by Kathleen Luft]. — 1st English language ed.
　　　　p.　cm. — (Barron's nature guide)
　　Includes bibliographical references and index.
　　ISBN 0-8120-1777-3
　　1. Minerals. 2. Minerals—Collection and preservation.
I. Title. II. Series.
QE372.2.H6413　1994
549—dc20
　　　　　　　　　　　　　　　　93-40790
　　　　　　　　　　　　　　　　CIP

▶ **Photo, pages 238–239:** Crocoite crystals up to almost $1/2$ inch (1 cm) in size, from the well-known Callenberg site in Saxony (Germany).

The Seven Crystal Systems

Isometric (cubic)

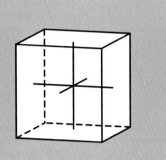

All three axes of the system of axes are equal in length and at right angles to each other.

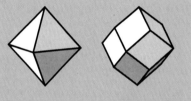

Fluorite

Tetragonal

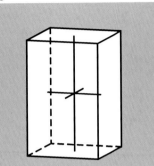

Two axes of the system of axes are equal in length, while the third is longer or shorter than the other two. All three are at right angles to each other.

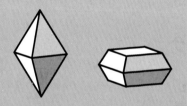

Scheelite

← Pocket